Alfred's Basic Piano Li

Piano

Notespeller Book
Complete Levels 2 & 3

Gayle Kowalchyk • E. L. Lancaster

Cover illustration and interior art by Russ Cohen

Instructions for Use

1. This NOTESPELLER is designed to be used with Alfred's Basic Piano Library, COMPLETE LEVELS 2 & 3 Lesson Book. It can also serve as an effective supplement for other piano methods.

2. This book is coordinated page-by-page with the LESSON BOOK, and assignments are ideally made according to the instructions in the upper right corner of each page of the NOTESPELLER.

3. This NOTESPELLER reinforces note reading concepts presented in the LESSON BOOK through written exercises. Note and interval identification exercises are presented throughout the book to provide the necessary systematic reinforcement for the student.

Gayle Kowalchyk
E. L. Lancaster

Contents

Use with Alfred's Basic Piano Library COMPLETE LESSON BOOK, Levels 2 & 3, pages 2–3.

Middle C and Middle D Positions (Review)

1. Write the missing notes on the staff from the MIDDLE C POSITION and the MIDDLE D POSITION. Use WHOLE NOTES.

2. Write the name of each note in the square below it.

Use with page 4.

Line Notes on the Grand Staff (Review)

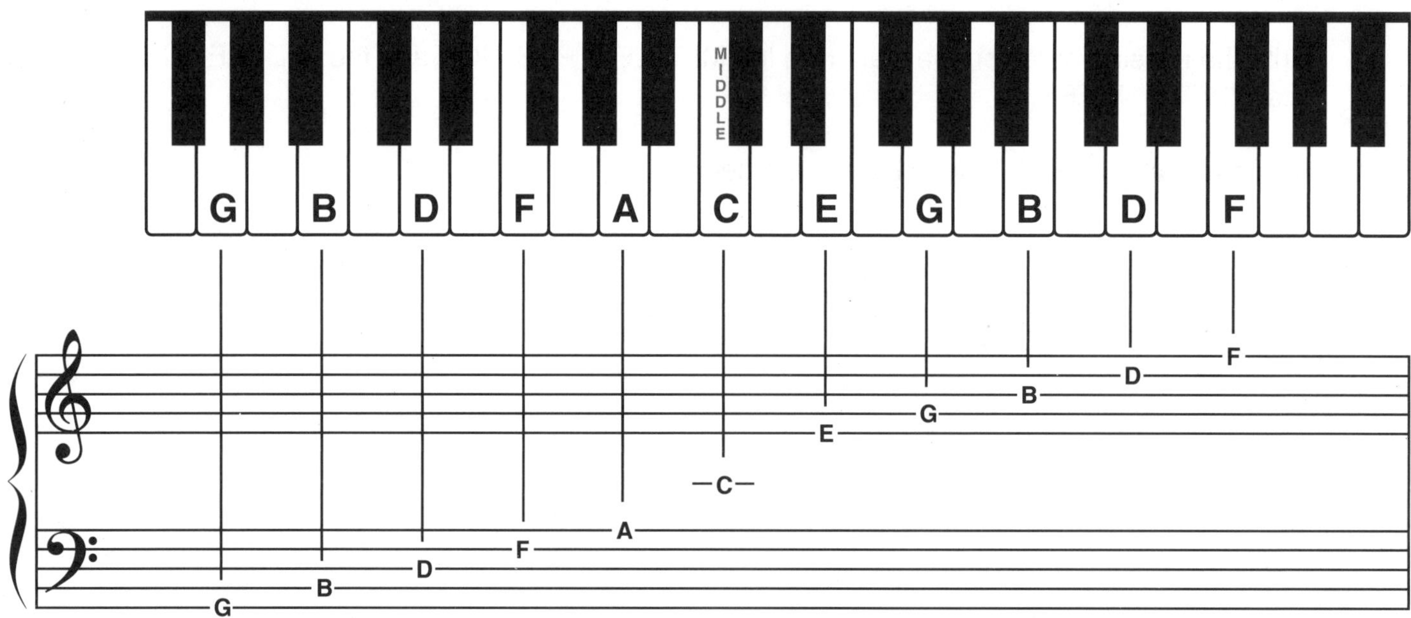

1. Write the names of the line notes on the grand staff. Begin with the bass staff.

2. Write the name of each note in the square below it.

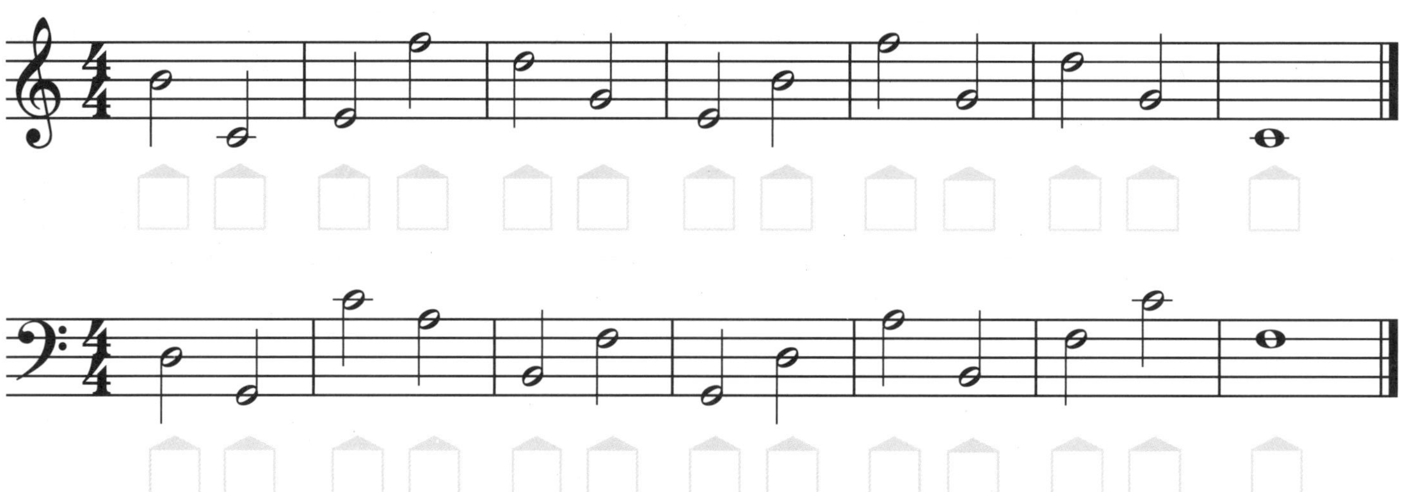

Use with page 5.

Space Notes on the Grand Staff (Review)

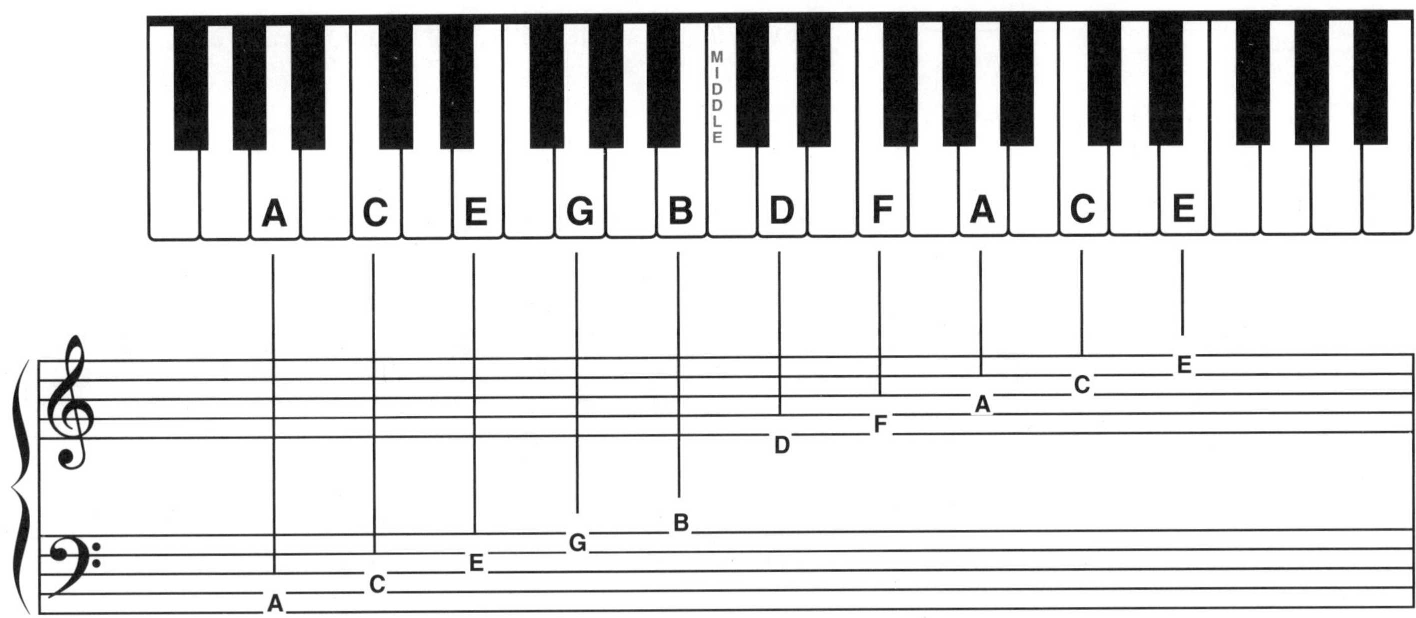

1. Write the names of the space notes on the grand staff. Begin with the bass staff.

2. Write the name of each note in the square below it.

Measuring 6ths

Use with pages 6–7.

When you skip 4 white keys, the interval is a **6th.**

6ths are written LINE-SPACE or SPACE-LINE.

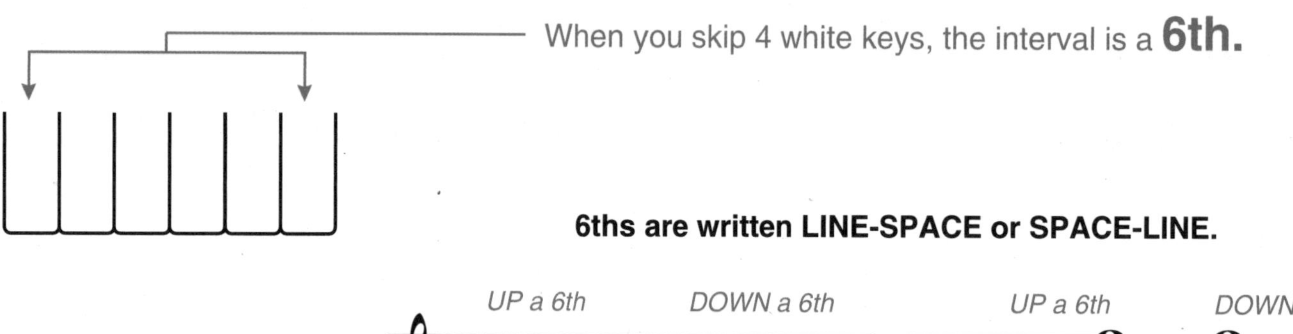

1. Write a half note UP a 6th from each C and DOWN a 6th from each A on the staffs below.
2. Write the name of each note in the square below it—then play and say the note name.

3. Write a whole note ABOVE the given note in each measure below to make the indicated harmonic interval.
4. Write the names of the notes in the squares. Write the name of the lower note in the lower square; the name of the higher note in the higher square.

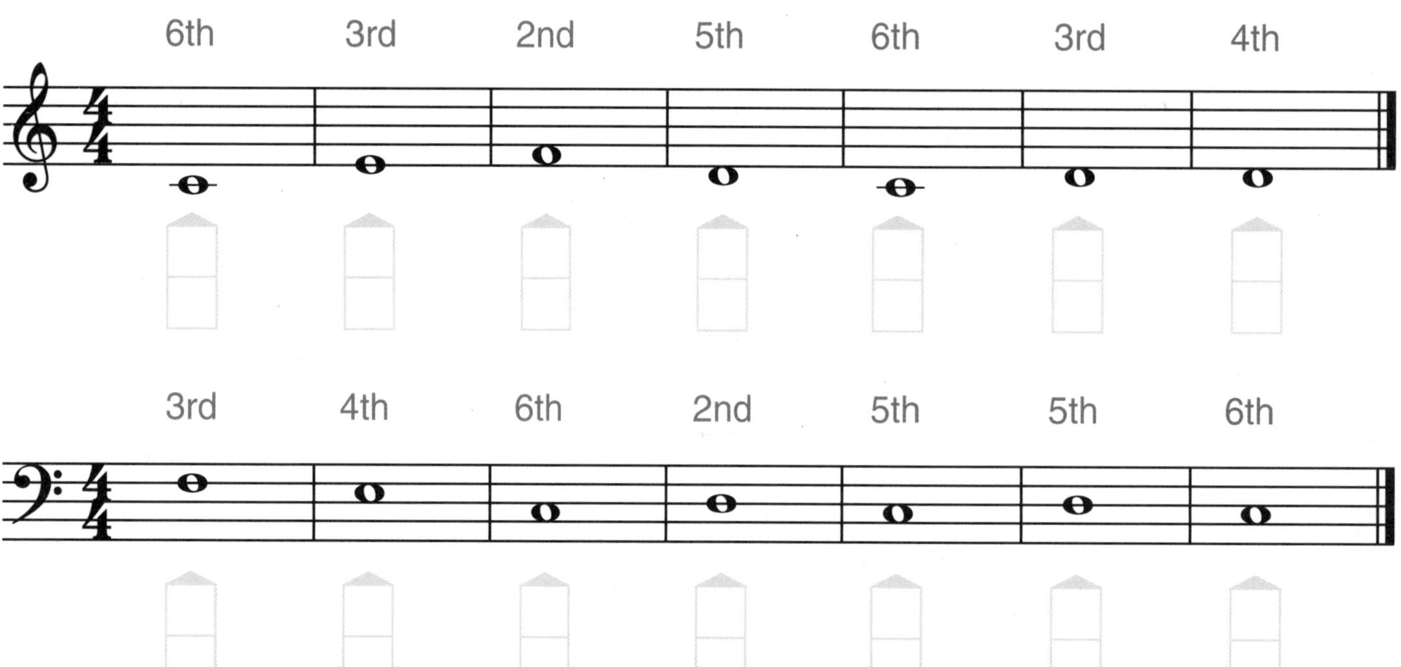

Use with pages 8–9.

Interval Review

1. Write a half note DOWN from the given note in each measure below to make the indicated melodic interval. Turn all the stems UP.

2. Write the name of each note in the square below it.

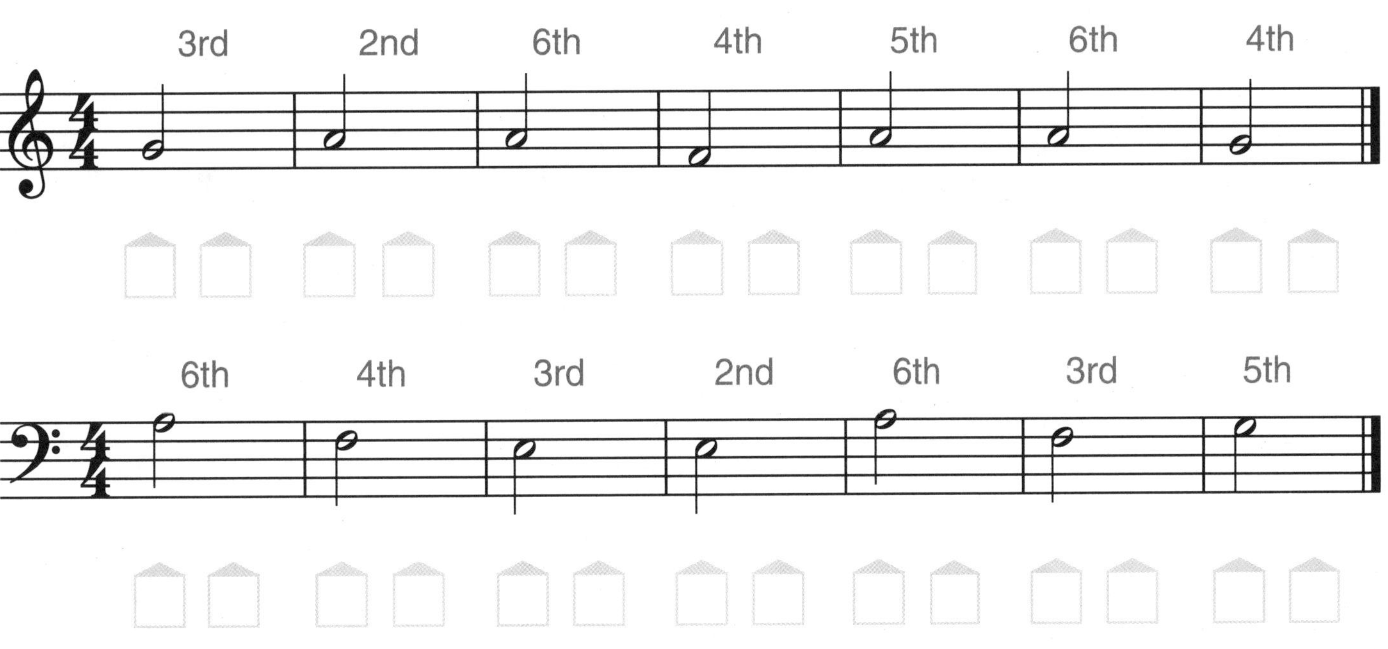

3. Write a whole note BELOW the given note to make the indicated harmonic interval.

4. Write the names of the notes in the squares below the staff. Write the name of the lower note in the lower square; the name of the higher note in the higher square.

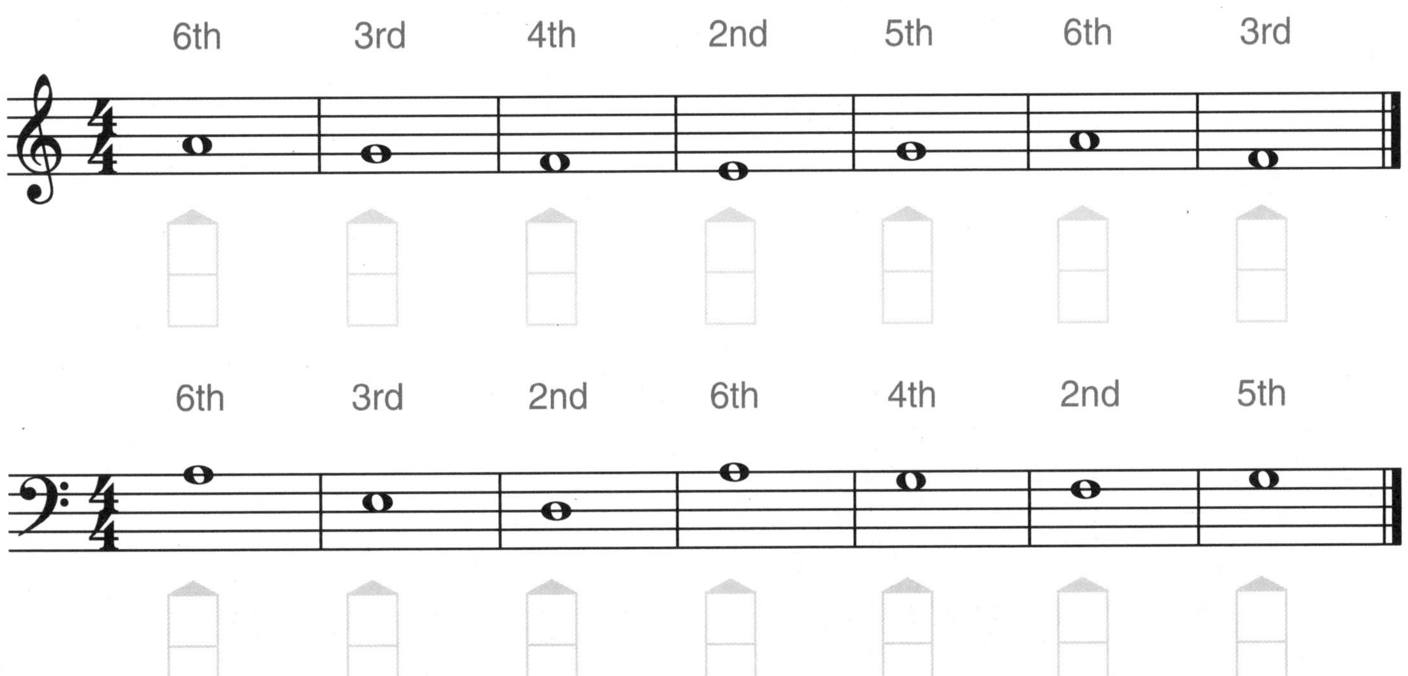

Interval Review

Use with pages 10–11.

1. Draw lines connecting the dots on the matching boxes.
2. Write the interval name (2, 3, 4, 5 or 6) on the line.

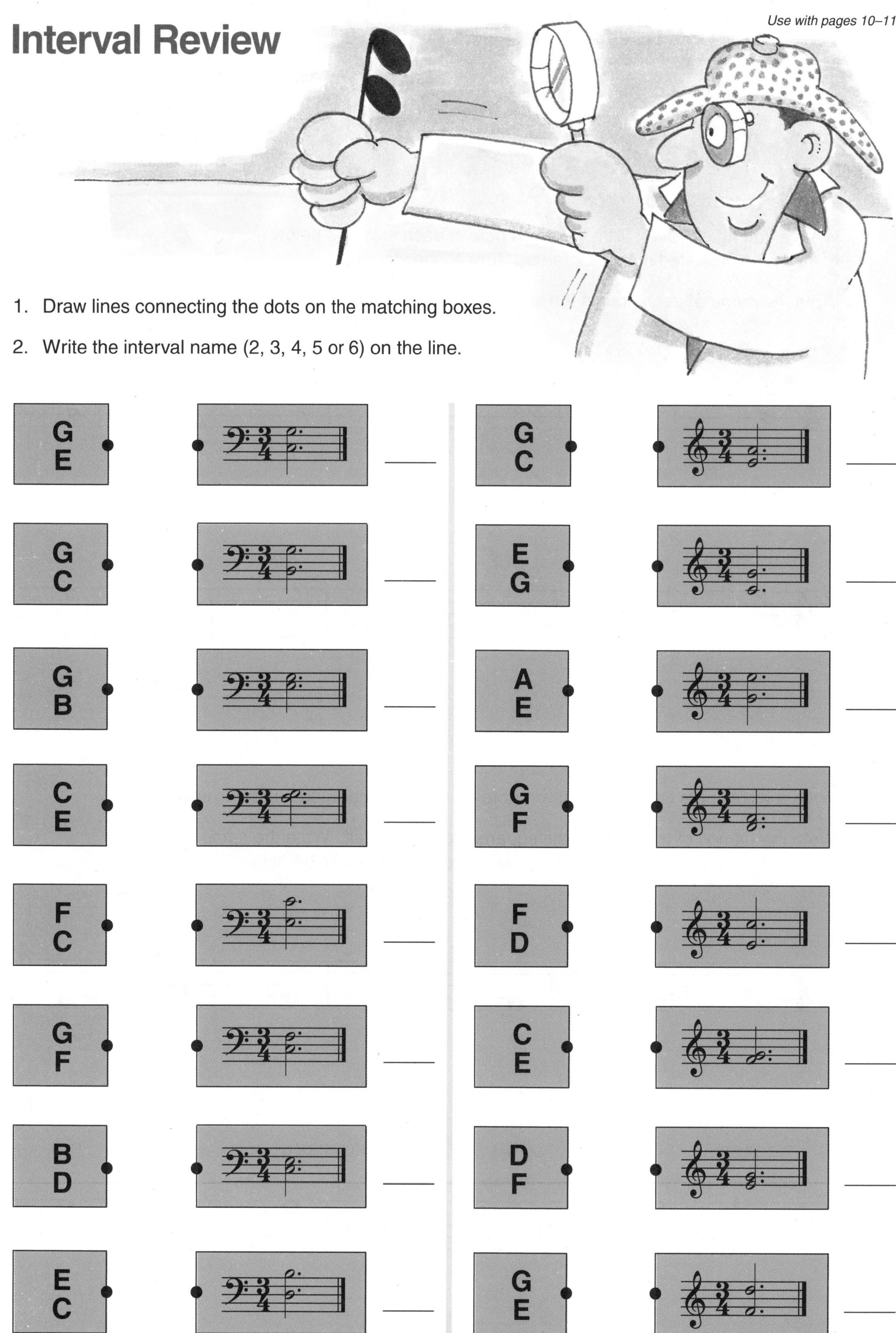

Use with pages 12–13.

Note Review

Solve the crossword puzzle by writing the names of the notes in the squares.

Interval Review

Use with pages 14–15.

1. Draw lines connecting the dots on the matching boxes.
2. Write the interval name (2, 3, 4, 5 or 6) on the line.

Use with page 16.

Measuring 7ths

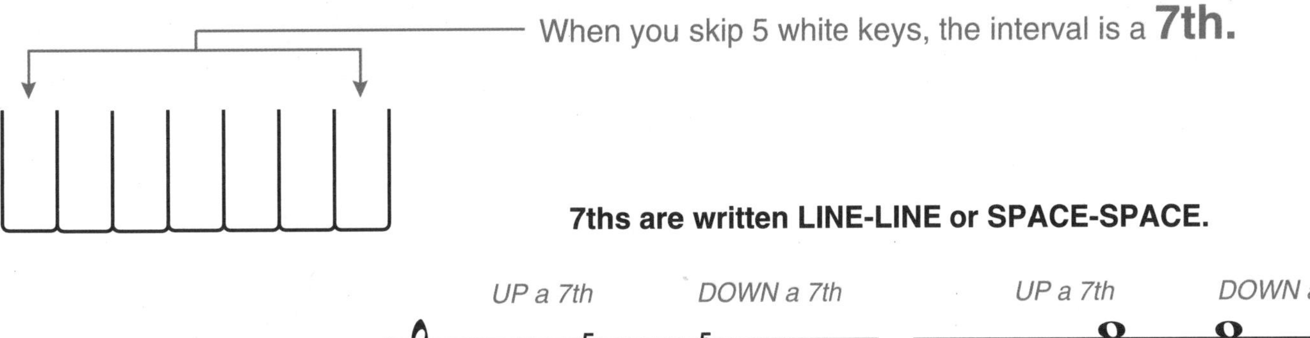

7ths are written LINE-LINE or SPACE-SPACE.

1. Write a half note UP a 7th from each C, and DOWN a 7th from each B on the staffs below.
2. Write the name of each note in the square below it—then play and say the note name.

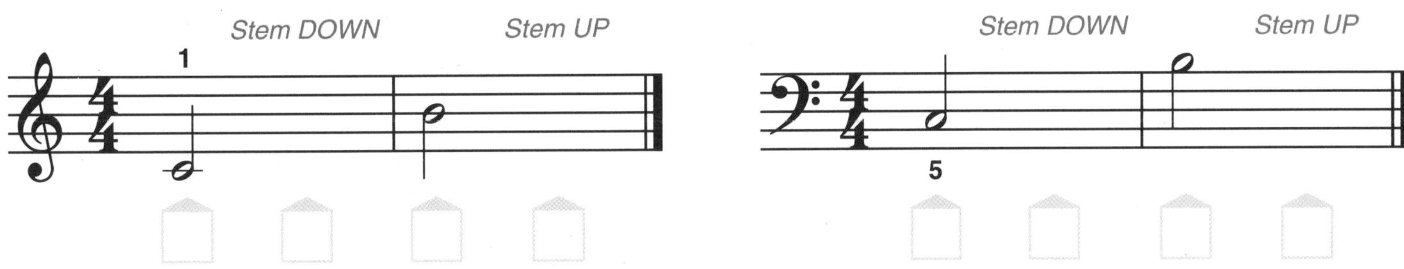

3. Write a whole note ABOVE the given note in each measure below to make the indicated harmonic interval.
4. Write the names of the notes in the squares. Write the name of the lower note in the lower square; the name of the higher note in the higher square.

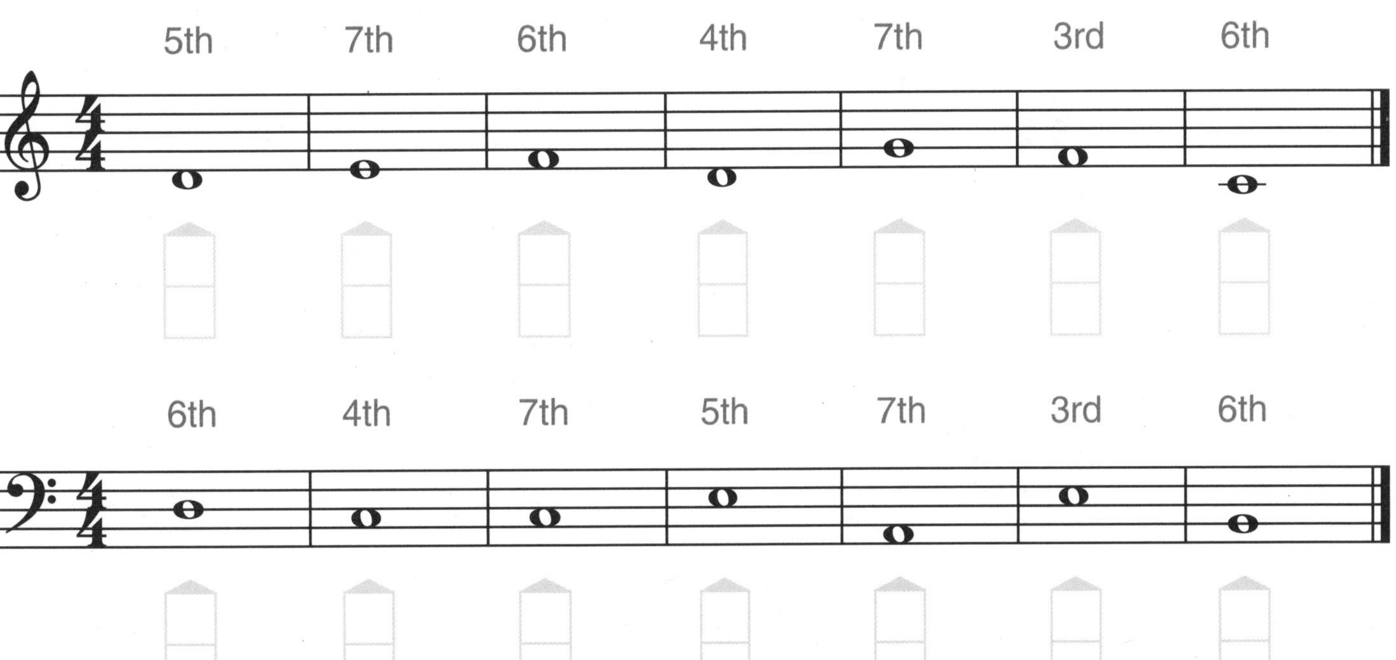

Use with page 17.

Interval Review

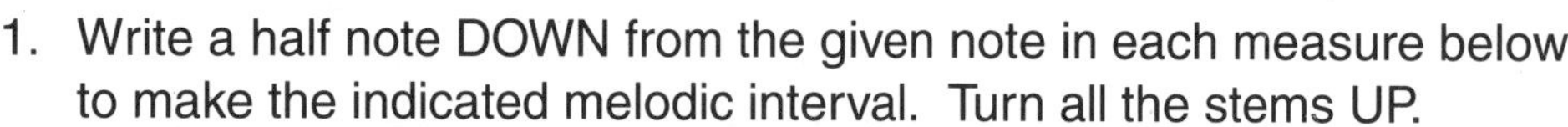

1. Write a half note DOWN from the given note in each measure below to make the indicated melodic interval. Turn all the stems UP.

2. Write the name of each note in the square below it.

3. Write a whole note BELOW the given note to make the indicated harmonic interval.

4. Write the names of the notes in the squares below the staff. Write the name of the lower note in the lower square; the name of the higher note in the higher square.

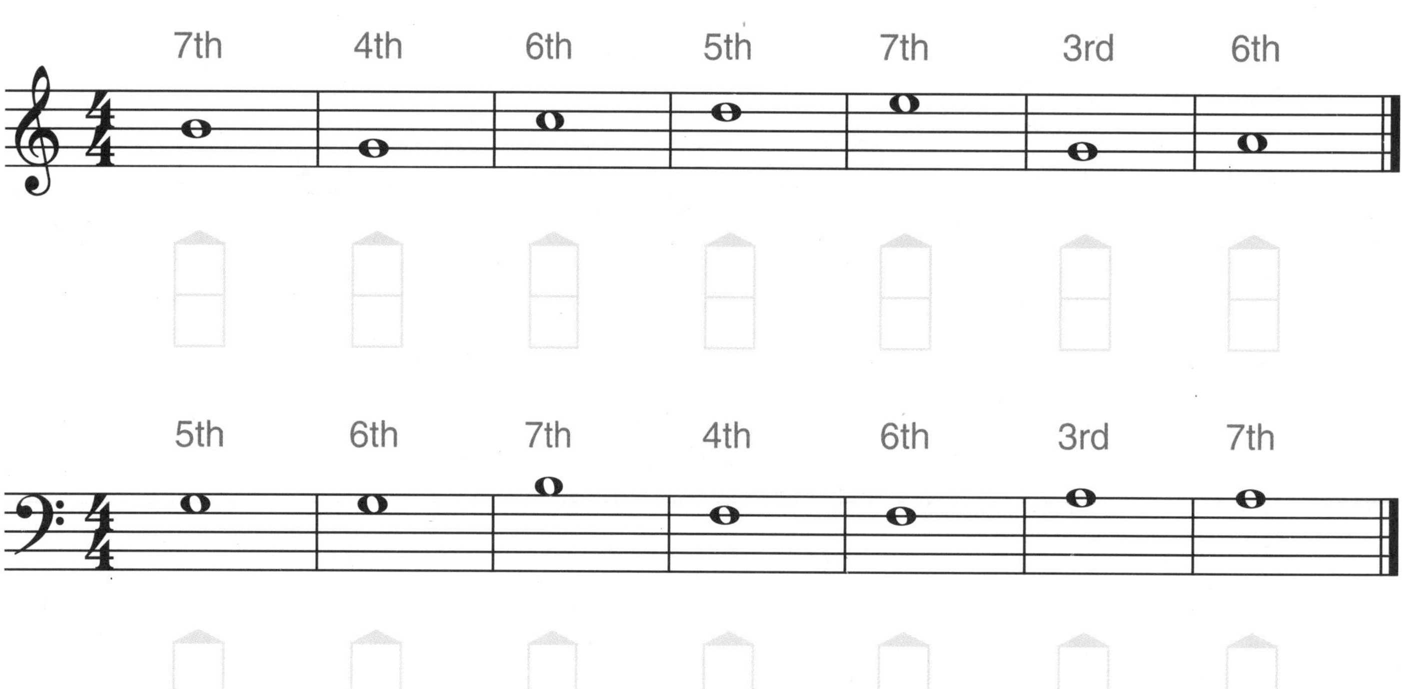

Use with pages 18–19.

The C Major Scale

1. Write the notes of the C MAJOR SCALE in the TREBLE staff over the squares. Use WHOLE NOTES.

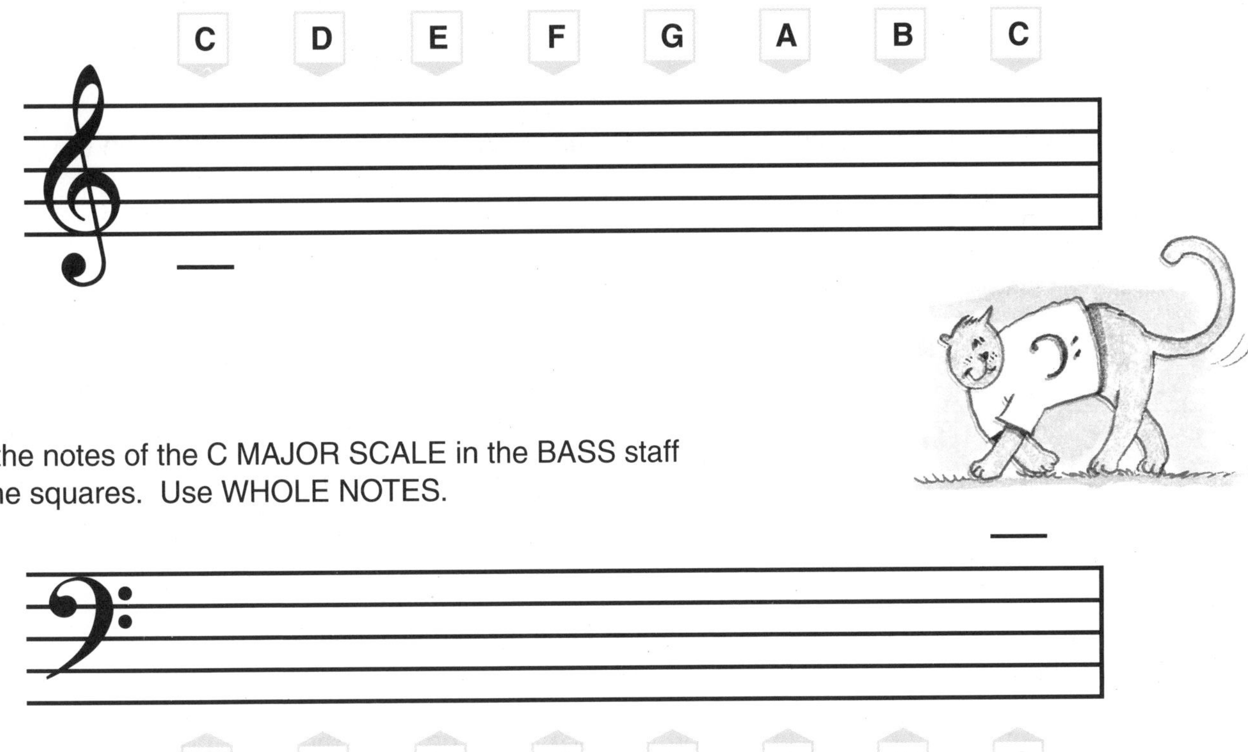

2. Write the notes of the C MAJOR SCALE in the BASS staff over the squares. Use WHOLE NOTES.

3. Write the name of each note in the square below it—then play and say the note names.

Use with page 20.

Measuring Octaves (8ths)

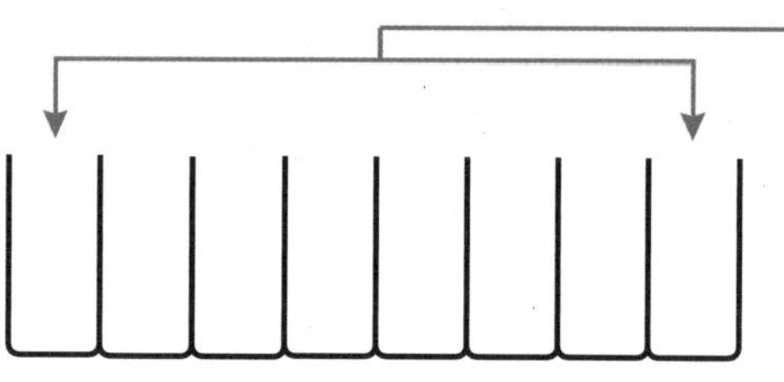

When you skip 6 white keys, the interval is an **Octave.**

Octaves are written LINE-SPACE or SPACE-LINE.

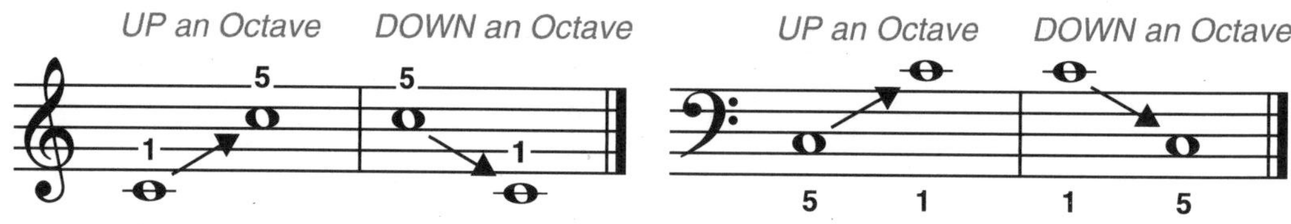

1. Write a half note UP an octave from each C and DOWN an octave from each C on the staffs below.
2. Write the name of each note in the square below it—then play and say the note name.

3. Write a whole note ABOVE the given note in each measure below to make the indicated harmonic interval.
4. Write the names of the notes in the squares. Write the name of the lower note in the lower square; the name of the higher note in the higher square.

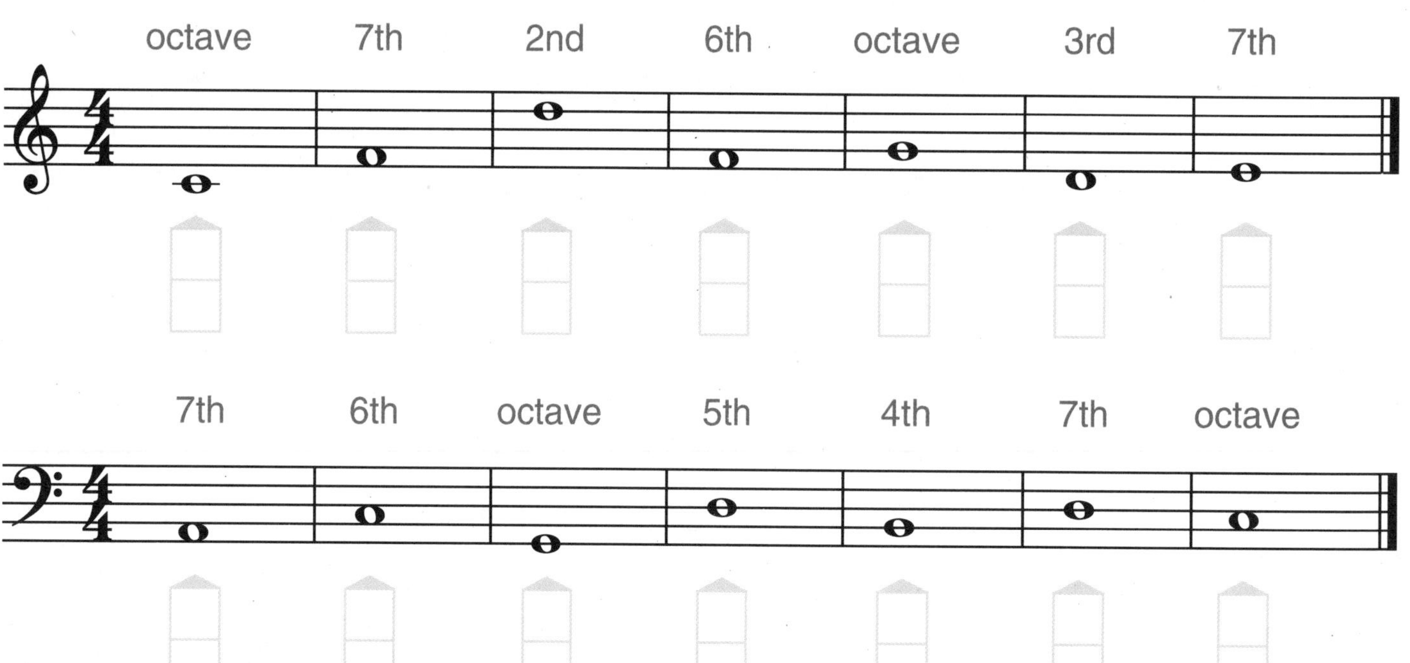

Use with page 21.

Note Review

1. Draw lines connecting the dots on the boxes containing the word in the center column to the dots on the matching boxes in bass clef in the left column.
2. Draw lines connecting the dots on the boxes containing the word in the center column to the dots on the matching boxes in treble clef in the right column.

Cabbage

Beg

Badge

Face

Add

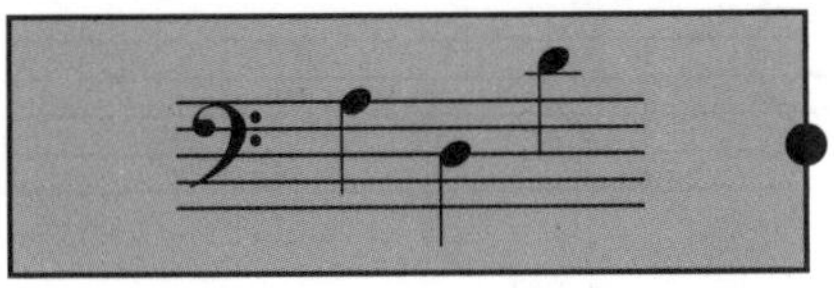

Cafe

Faced

Baggage

The G Major Scale

Use with pages 22–23.

1. Write the notes of the G MAJOR SCALE in the TREBLE staff under the squares. Use WHOLE NOTES.

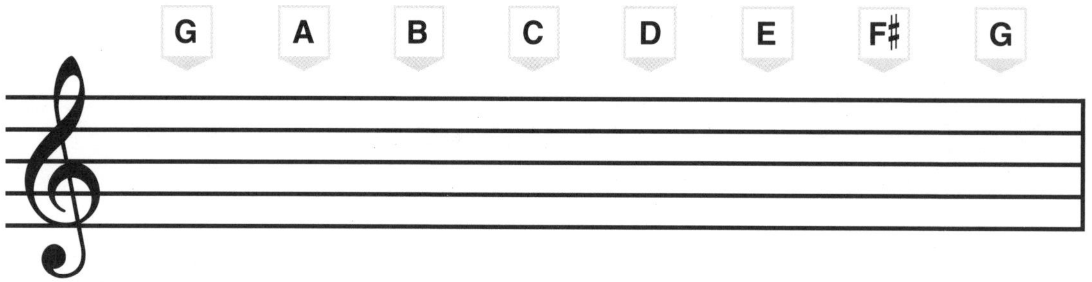

2. Write the notes of the G MAJOR SCALE in the BASS staff over the squares. Use WHOLE NOTES.

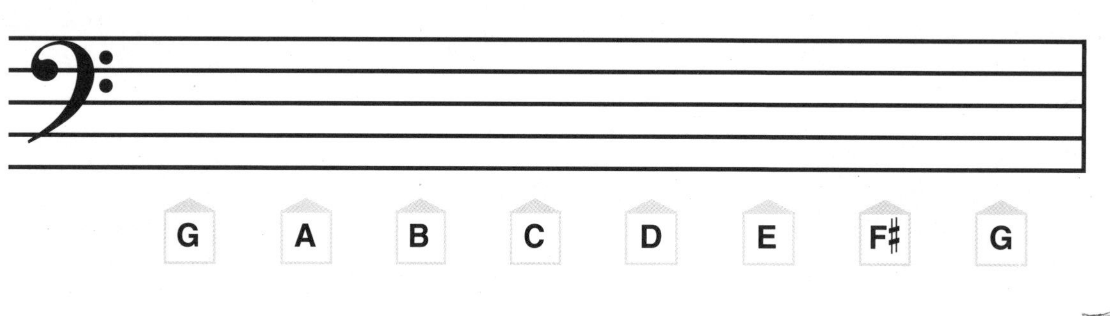

3. Write the name of each note in the square below it—then play and say the note names.

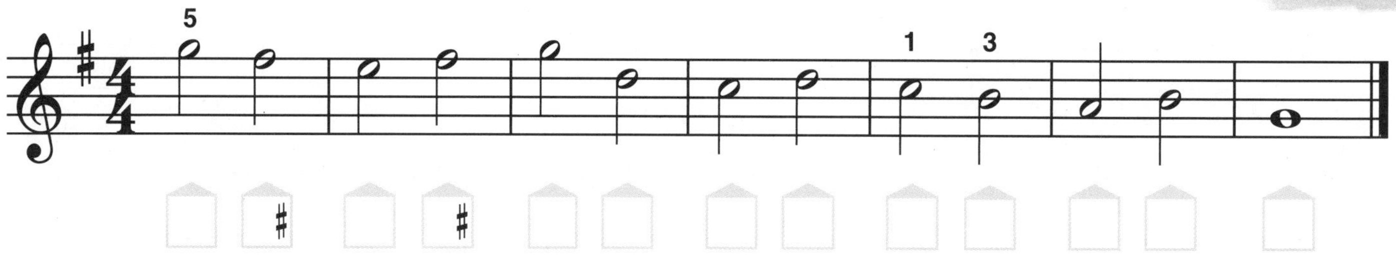

Use with page 24.

Triads

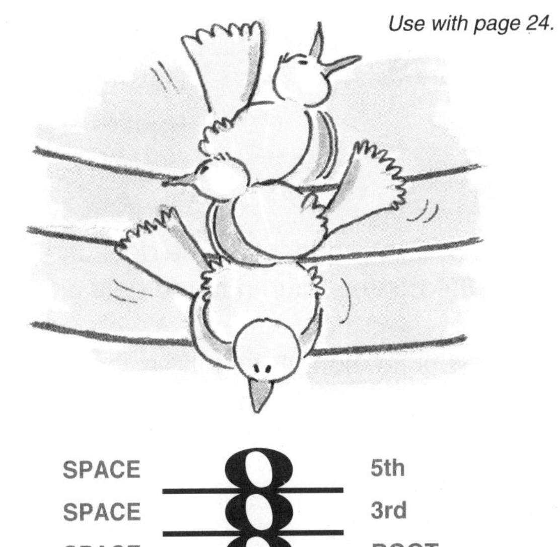

A TRIAD IS A 3-NOTE CHORD.

The ROOT is the note from which the triad gets its name.
The ROOT of a C triad is C.

Triads in **ROOT POSITION** (with the ROOT at the bottom) always look like this:

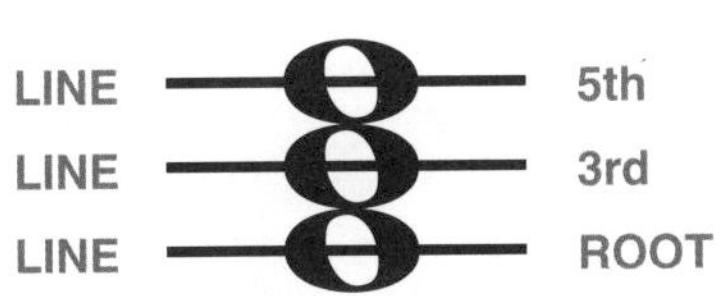

or this:

SPACE 5th
SPACE 3rd
SPACE ROOT

TRIADS MAY BE BUILT ON ANY NOTE OF ANY SCALE.

1. Circle the 1st, 3rd and 5th notes of each of the scales.
   These notes form a root position triad.

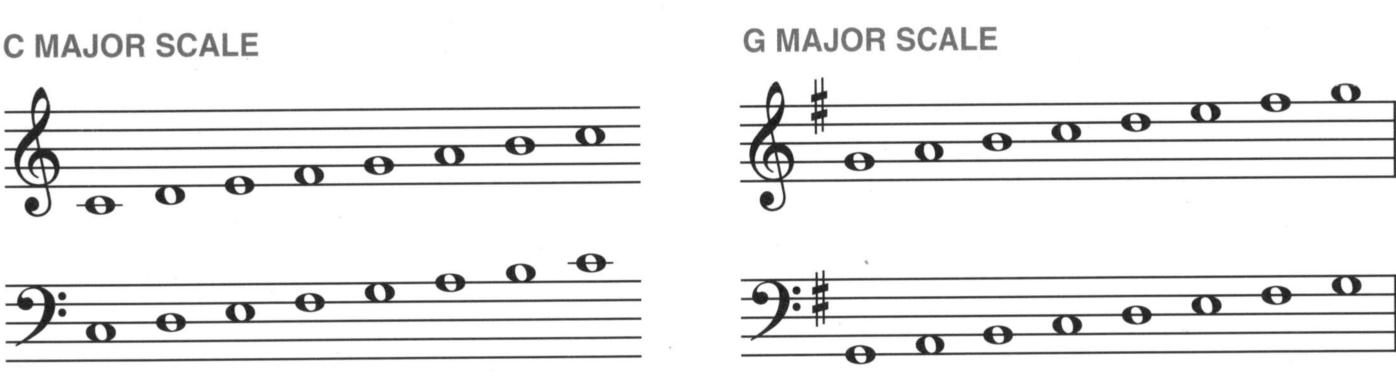

2. Write the names of the notes in each triad in the squares above the staff.
3. Circle each C and G triad.

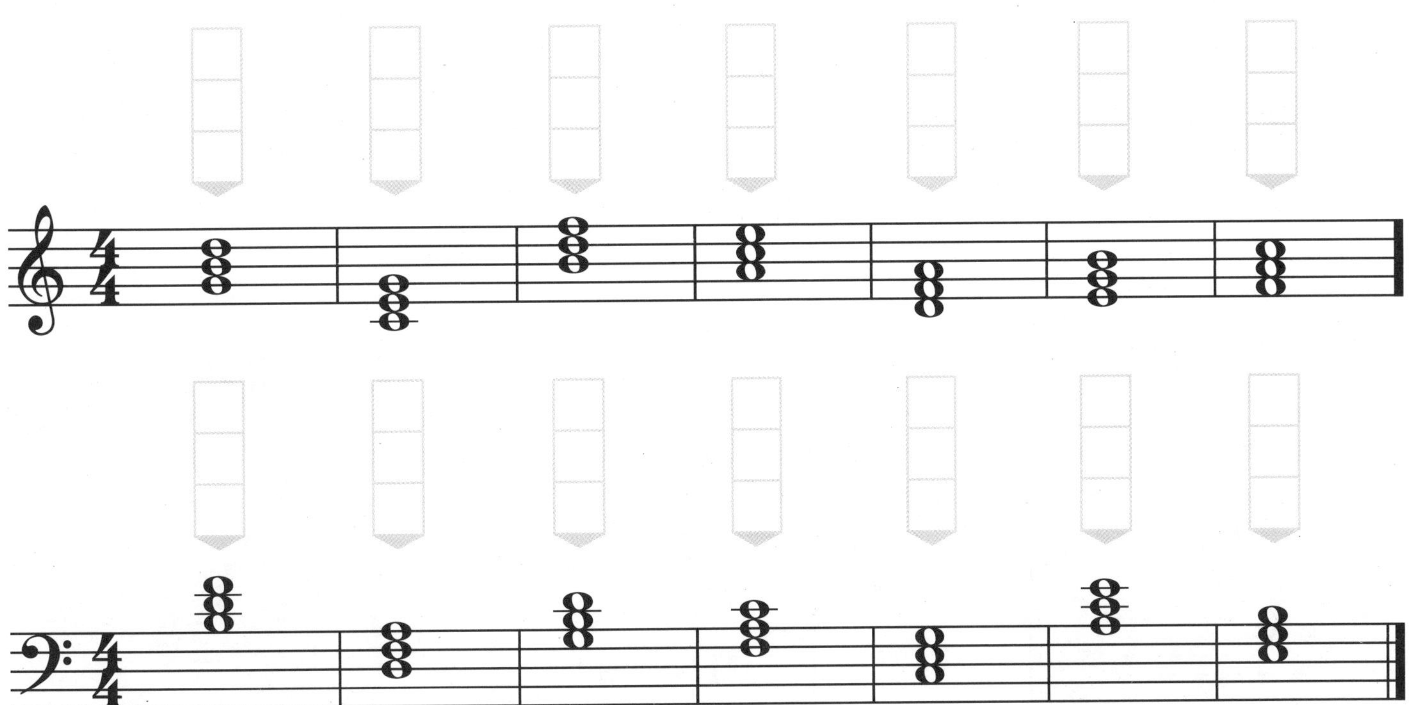

Triads

Use with page 25.

1. Draw lines connecting the dots on the boxes containing the note names of the triads in the center column to the dots on the matching boxes in bass clef in the left column.
2. Draw lines connecting the dots on the boxes containing the note names of the triads in the center column to the dots on the matching boxes in treble clef in the right column.

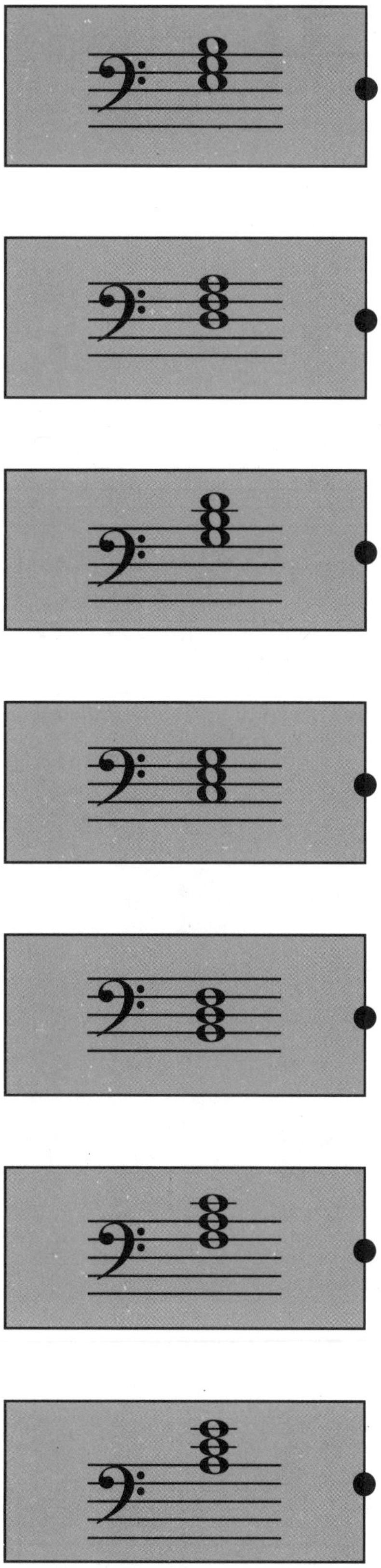

G
E
C

A
F
D

B
G
E

C
A
F

D
B
G

E
C
A

F
D
B

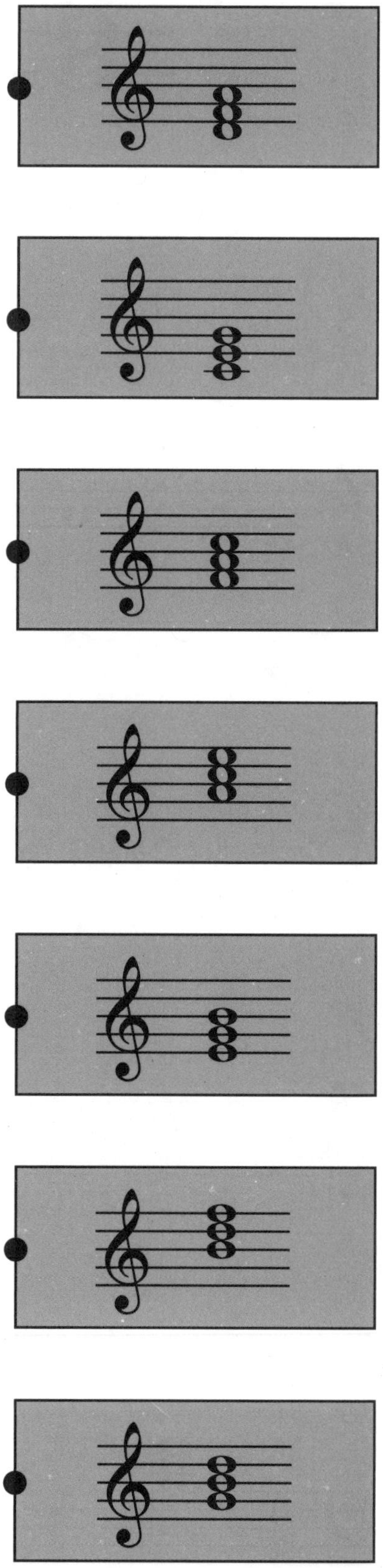

Use with pages 26–27.

Triads

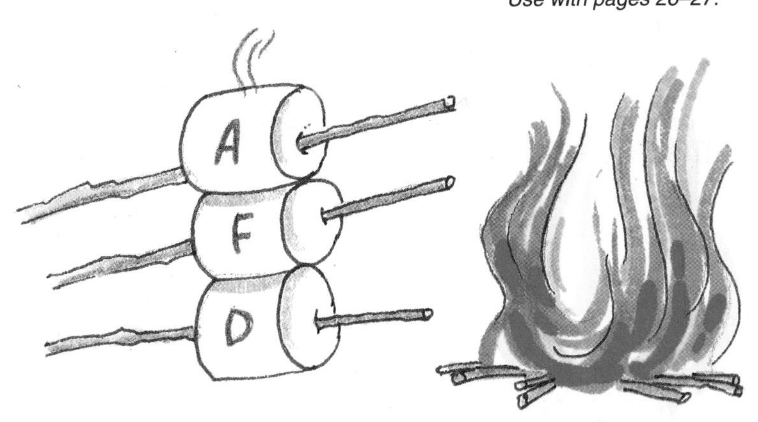

1. Circle the triad on the bass staff that matches the letter name of its root in the middle column.
2. Circle the triad on the treble staff that matches the letter name of its root in the middle column.

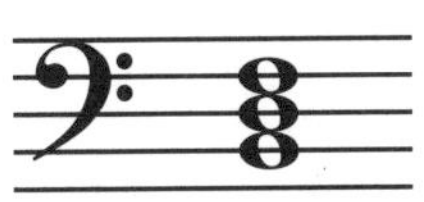

A

B

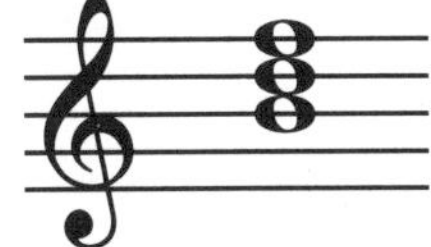

C

D

E

F

G

The Primary Triads

Use with pages 28–29.

The three most important triads in any key are those built on the 1st, 4th, & 5th notes of the scale. These are called the PRIMARY TRIADS of the key.

1. Circle the 1st, 4th and 5th notes of each of the scales below.
   These notes are the roots of the primary triads.

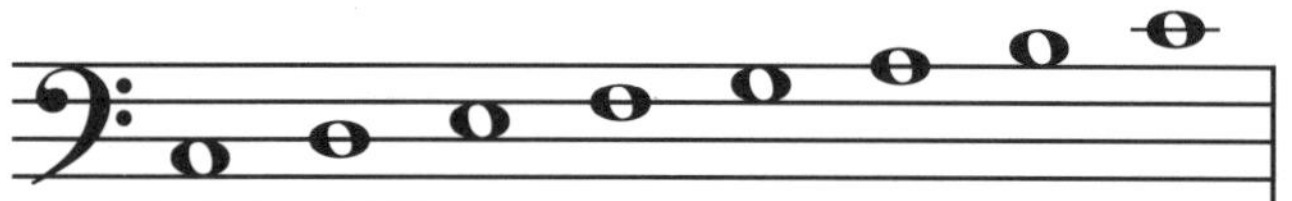

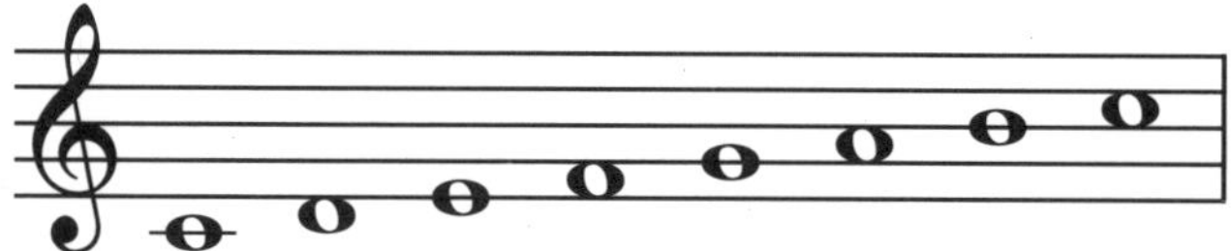

To make the chord progressions easier to play and sound better, the **IV** and **V** chords may be played in other positions by moving one or more of the higher chord tones down an octave.

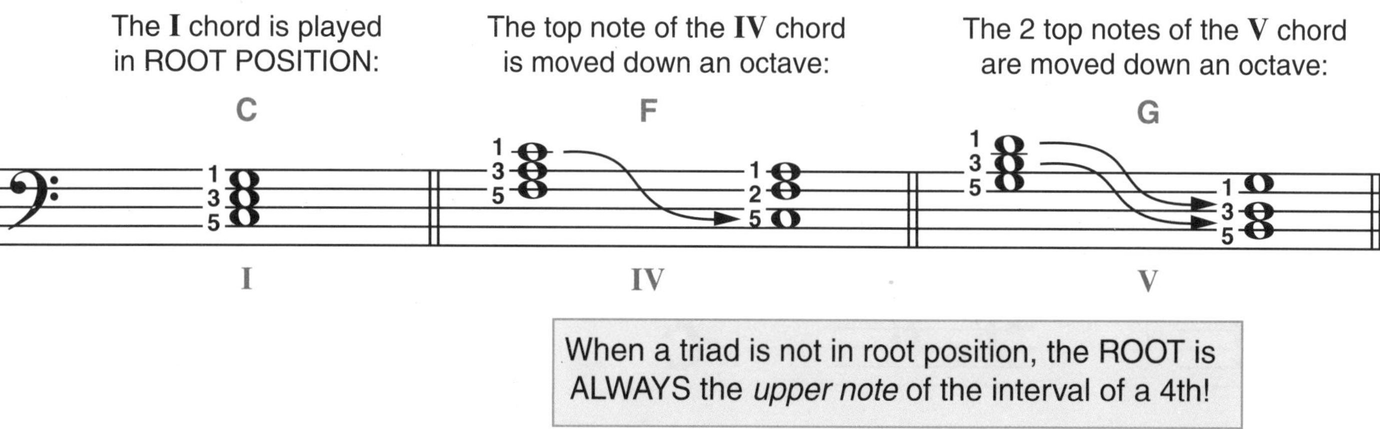

2. Write the names of the notes in each chord in the squares above the staff.
3. Circle the root of each chord on the staff.
4. Write the name of the chord (**I**, **IV** or **V**) on the line below the staff.

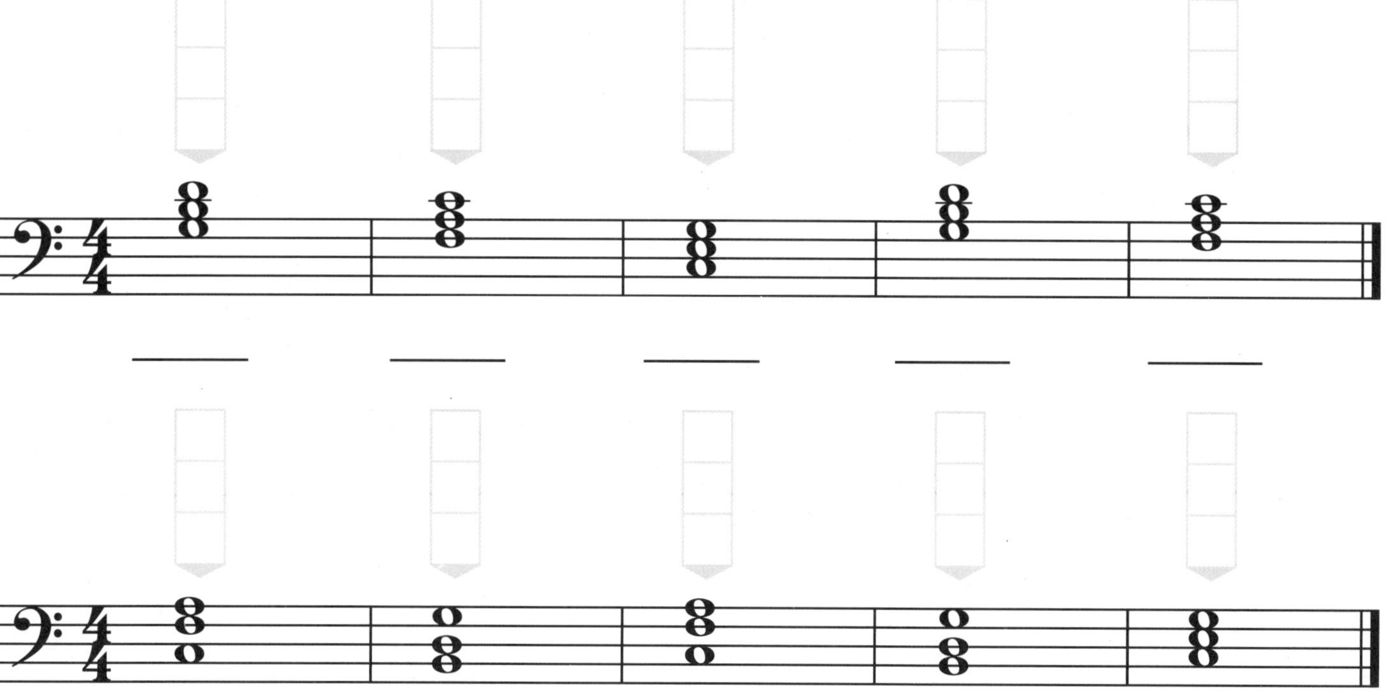

Use with pages 30–31.

The Primary Chords in C Major

In many pieces a **V7** CHORD is used instead of a **V** TRIAD.
To make a **V7** chord, a note an interval of a 7th above the root is added to the **V** triad.

V7 built on the 5th note of the C SCALE:

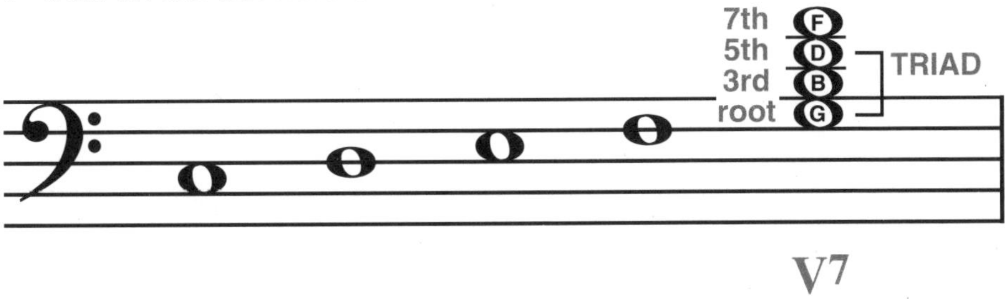

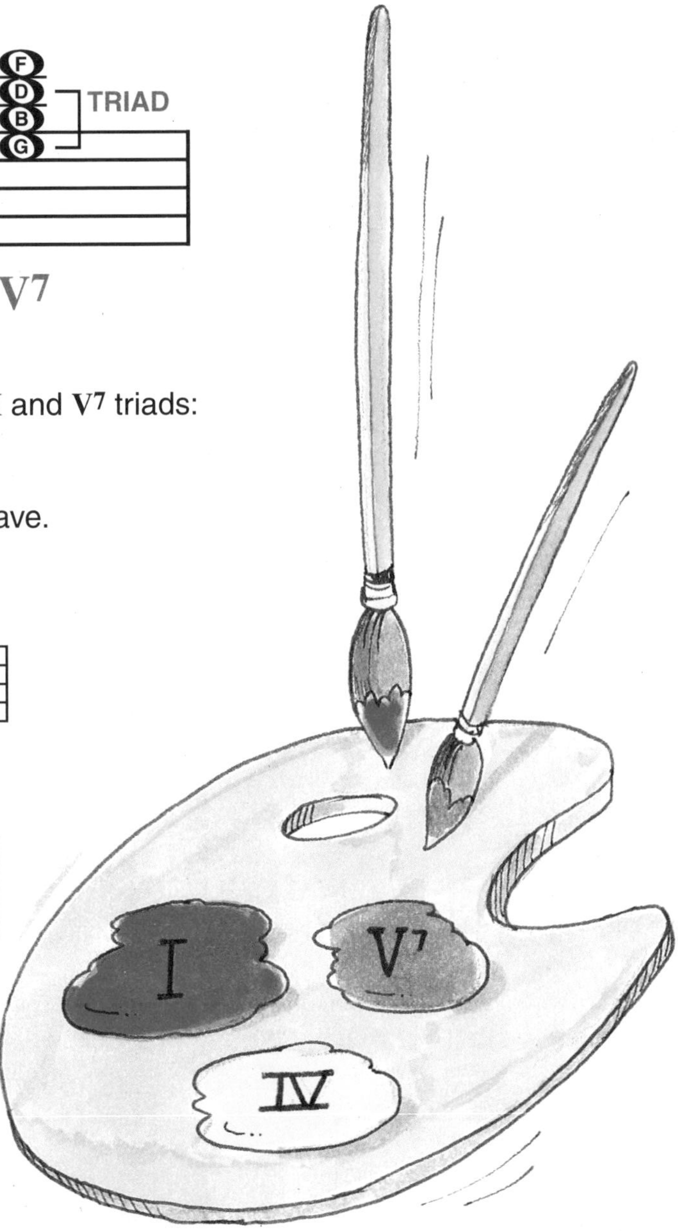

7th F
5th D
3rd B
root G
TRIAD

V7

To have a smoother and easier progression with the **I** and **V7** triads:

- The 5th (D) is omitted.
- The 3rd (B) and 7th (F) are moved down an octave.

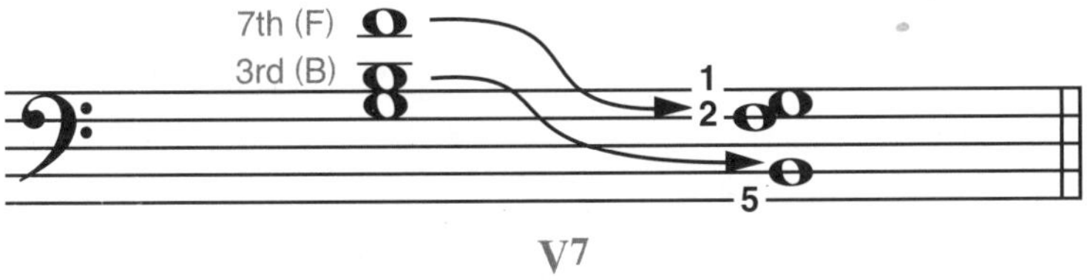

7th (F)
3rd (B)
1
2
5

V7

When a 7th chord is not in root position, the ROOT is ALWAYS the *upper note* of the interval of a 2nd!

1. Write the names of the notes in each chord in the squares above the staff.
2. Circle the root of each chord on the staff.
3. Write the name of the chord (**I**, **IV** or **V7**) on the line below the staff.

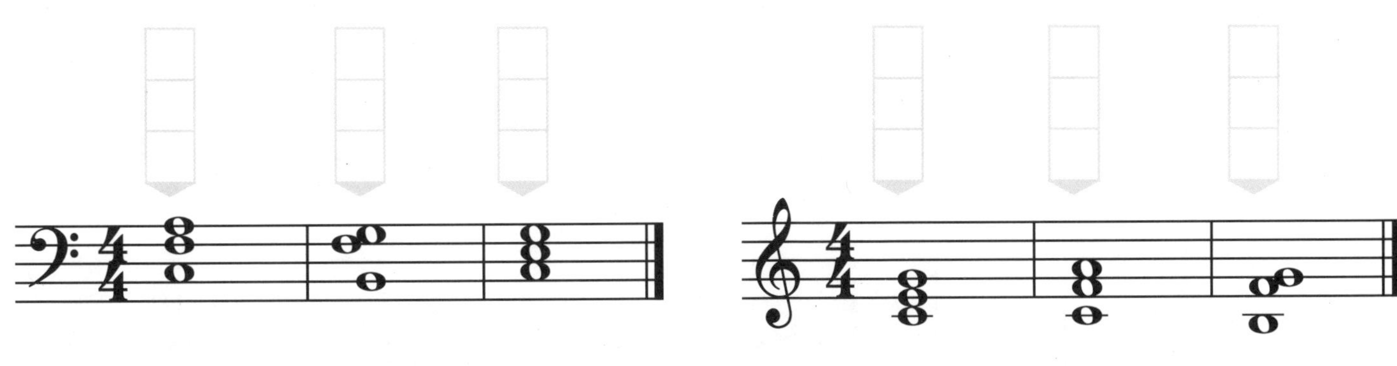

The Primary Chords in G Major

Use with pages 32–33.

1. Write the names of the notes in each chord in the squares above the staff.
2. Circle the root of each chord on the staff.
3. Write the name of the chord (**I**, **IV** or **V7**) on the line below the staff.

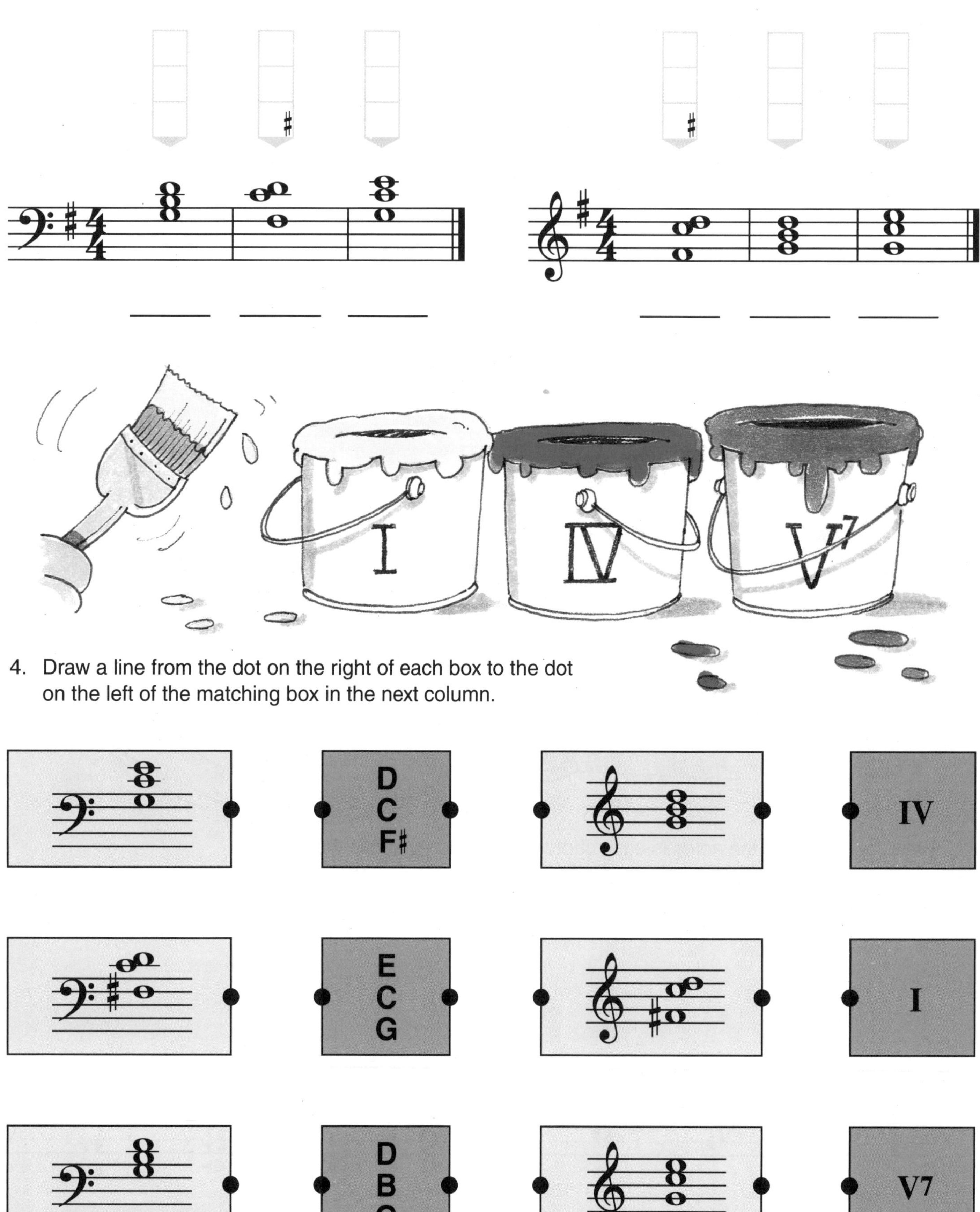

4. Draw a line from the dot on the right of each box to the dot on the left of the matching box in the next column.

Use with pages 34–35.

Block and Broken Chords

1. Draw lines connecting the dots on the boxes containing the note names in the center column to the dots on the matching boxes containing block chords in the left column.
2. Draw lines connecting the dots on the boxes containing the note names in the center column to the dots on the matching boxes containing broken chords in the right column.

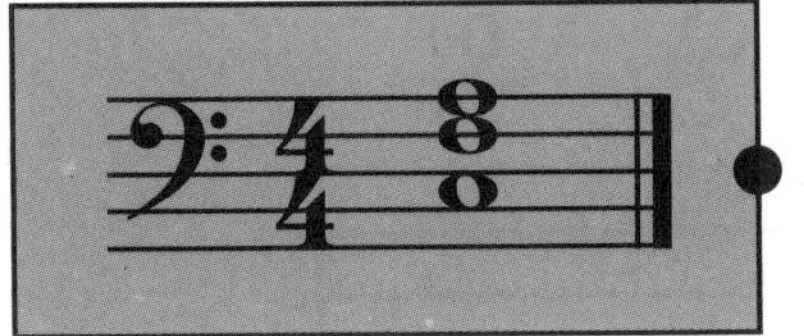

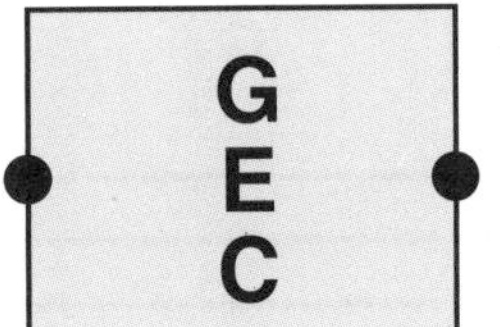

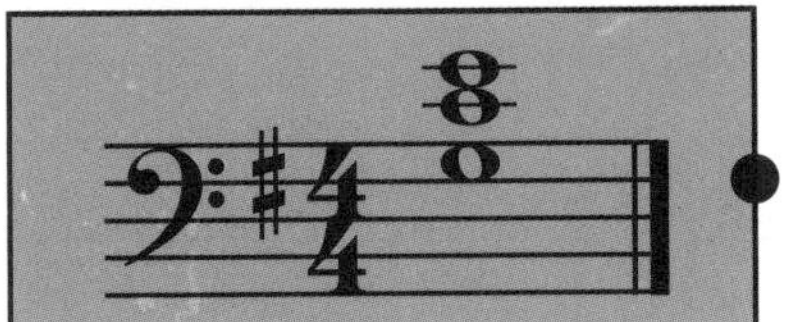

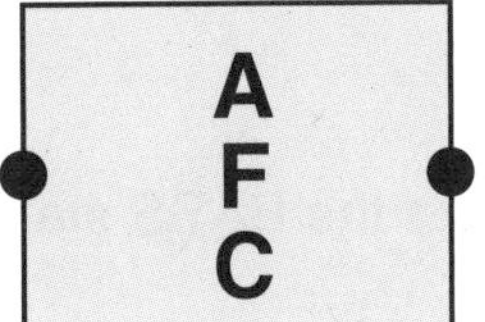

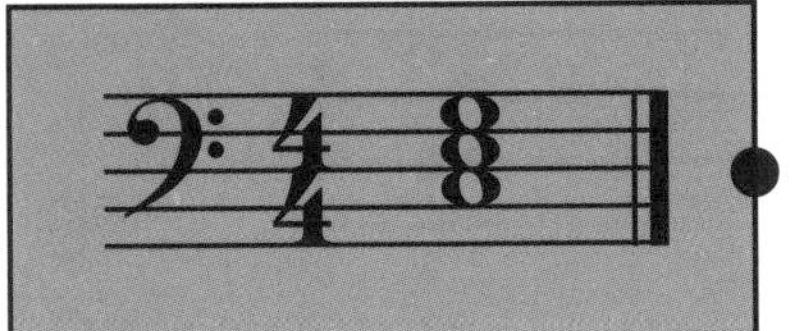

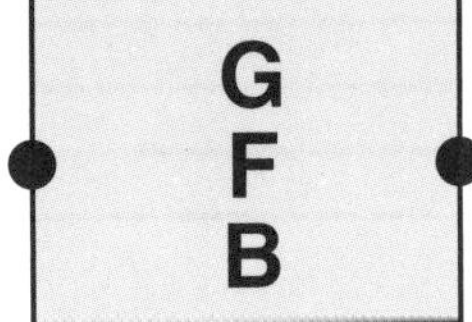

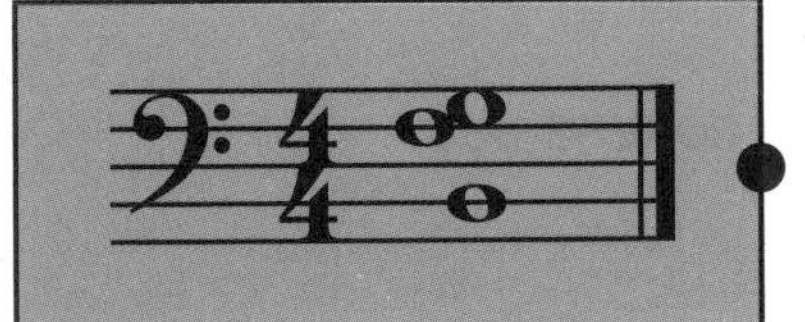

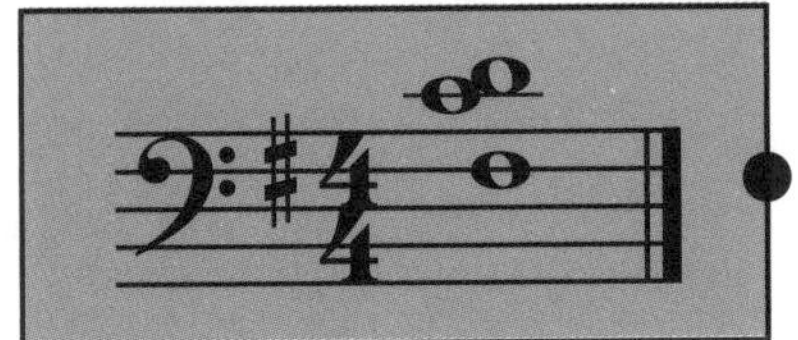

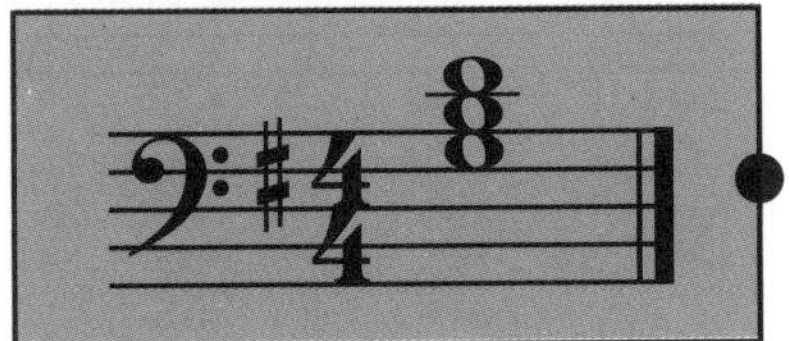

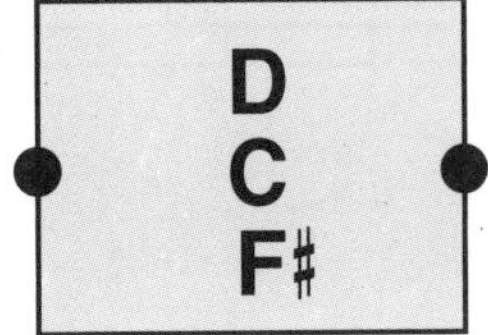

The D Major Scale

Use with pages 36–37.

1. Write the notes of the D MAJOR SCALE in the TREBLE staff under the squares. Use WHOLE NOTES.

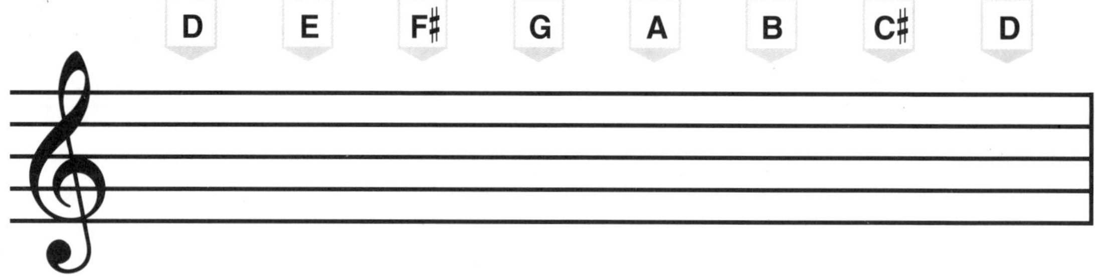

2. Write the notes of the D MAJOR SCALE in the BASS staff over the squares. Use WHOLE NOTES.

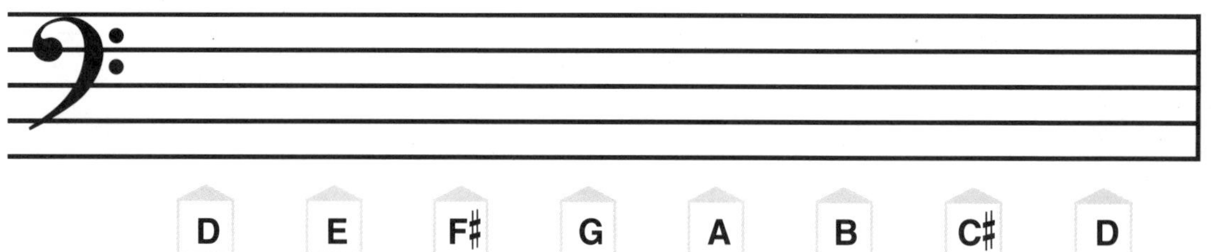

3. Write the name of each note in the square below it—then play and say the note names.

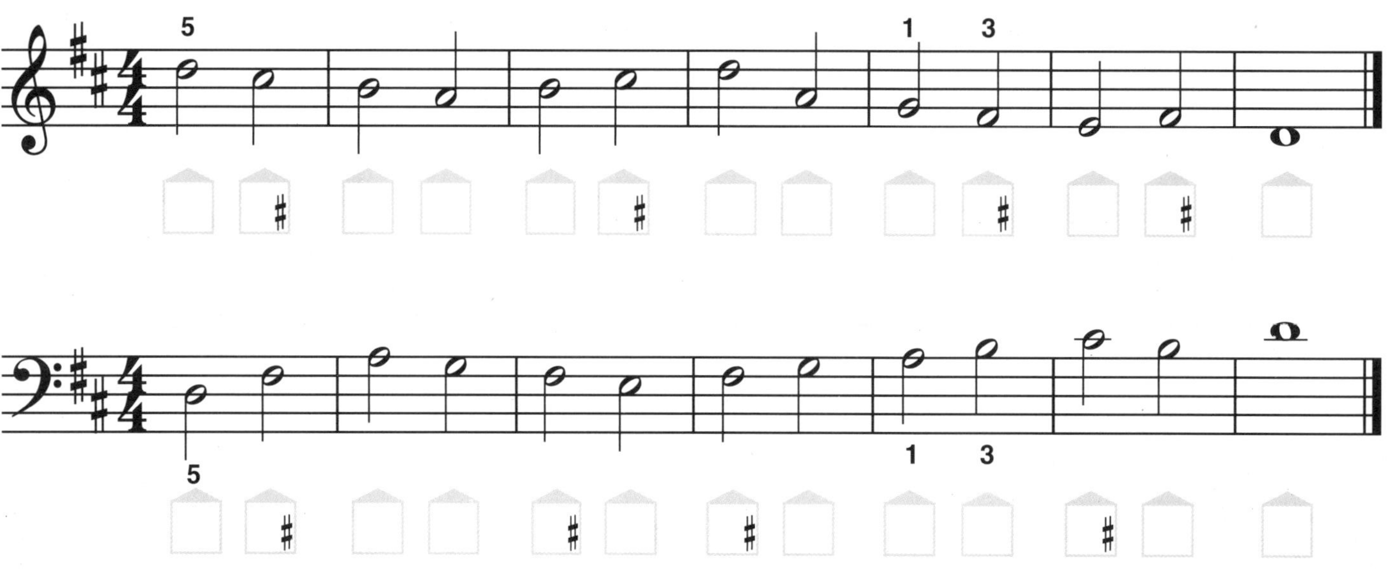

Use with pages 38–39.

The Primary Chords in D Major

1. Write the names of the notes in each chord in the squares above the staff.
2. Circle the root of each chord on the staff.
3. Write the name of the chord (**I**, **IV** or **V7**) on the line below the staff.

4. Draw a line from the dot on the right of each box to the dot on the left of the matching box in the next column.

Chord Review

Use with pages 40–41.

Draw a line from the dot on the right of each box to the dot on the left of the matching box in the next column.

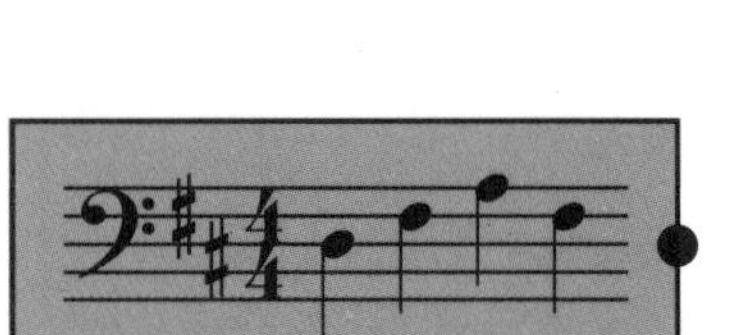
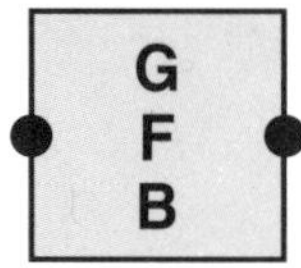

Key of C
I

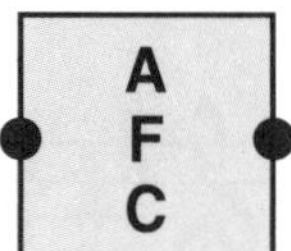

Key of C
IV

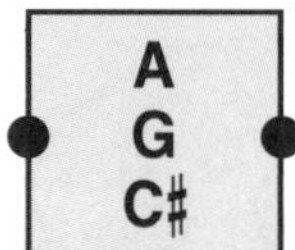

Key of C
V7

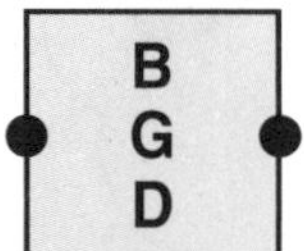

Key of G
I

Key of G
IV

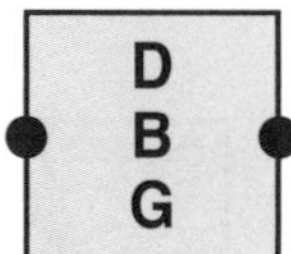

Key of G
V7

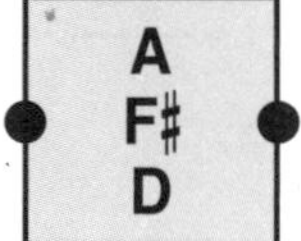

Key of D
I

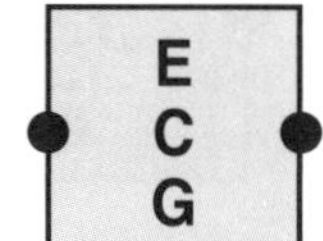

Key of D
IV

Key of D
V7

Use with pages 42–43.

Primary Chords Review

1. Circle the chord on the bass staff that matches its name in the middle column.
2. Circle the triad on the treble staff that matches its name in the middle column.

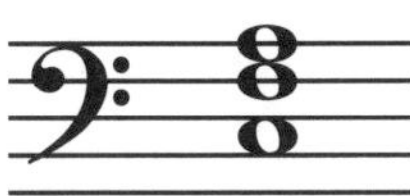

A^7

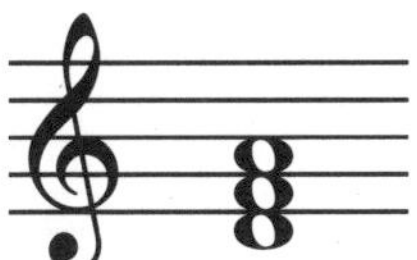

F

D

D^7

G

C

G^7

Interval Review

Use with pages 44–45.

1. Write a half note DOWN from the given note in each measure below to make the indicated melodic interval.
2. Write the name of each note in the square below it.

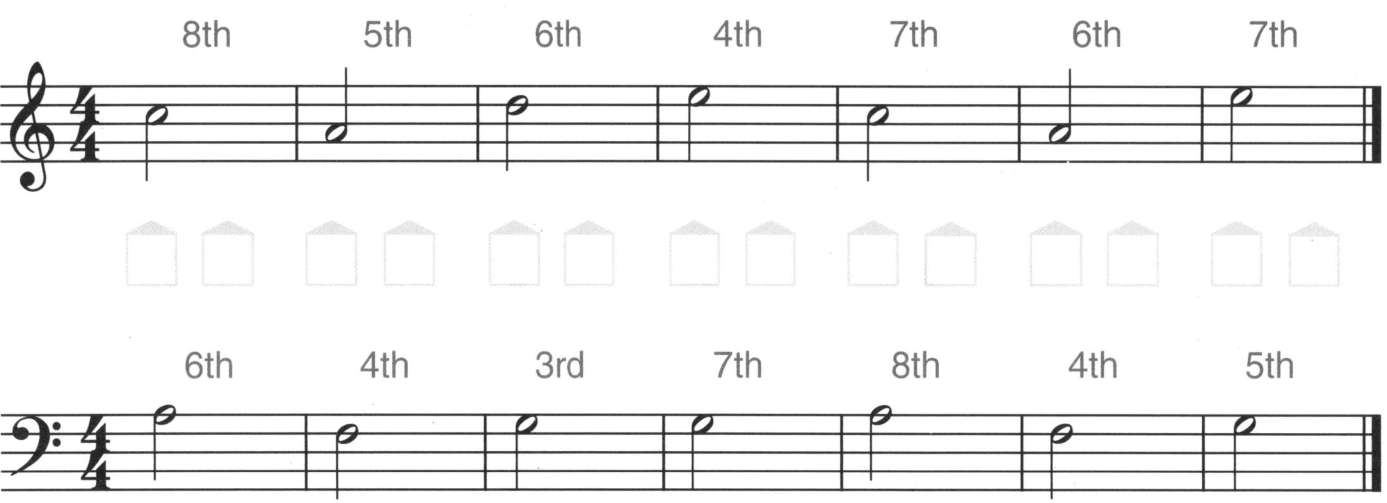

3. Write a whole note BELOW the given note to make the indicated harmonic interval.
4. Write the names of the notes in the squares below the staff. Write the name of the lower note in the lower square; the name of the higher note in the higher square.

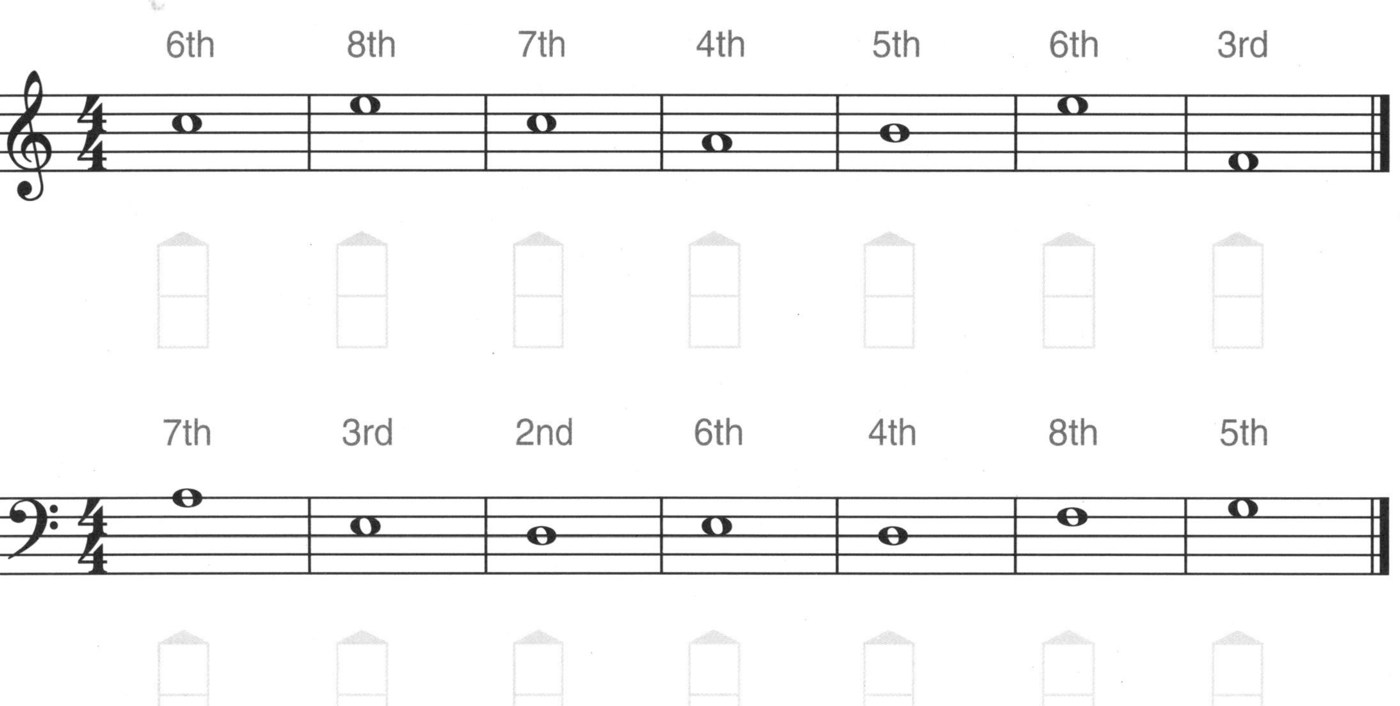

Use with pages 46–47.

Major Scale Review

1. Write the notes of the D MAJOR SCALE in the TREBLE staff under the squares.
   Use WHOLE NOTES.

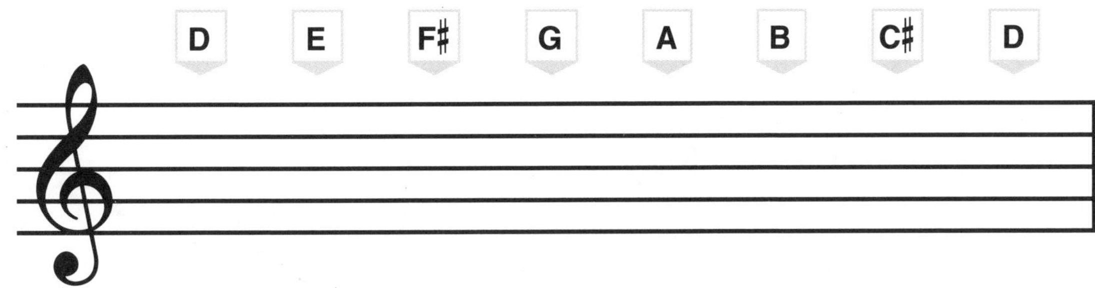

2. Write the notes of the D MAJOR SCALE in the BASS staff over the squares.
   Use WHOLE NOTES.

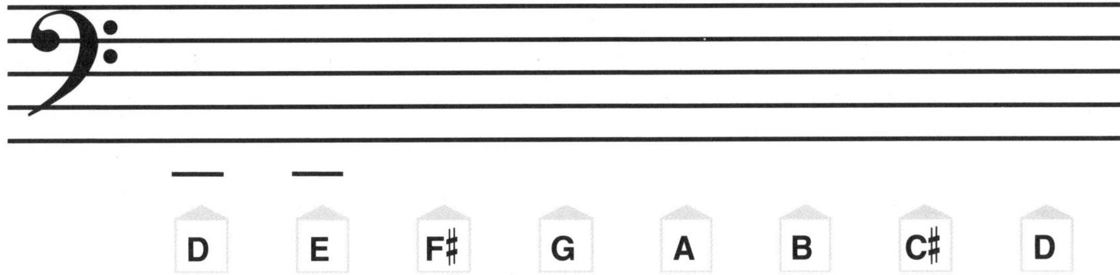

3. Write the notes of the C MAJOR SCALE in the BASS staff over the squares.
   Use WHOLE NOTES.

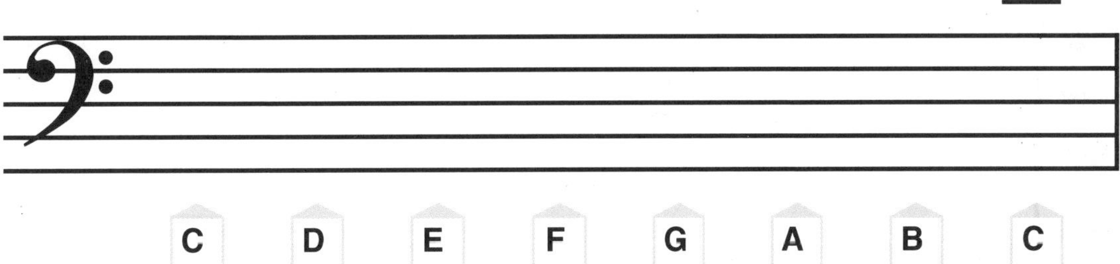

4. Write the notes of the G MAJOR SCALE in the TREBLE staff under the squares.
   Use WHOLE NOTES.

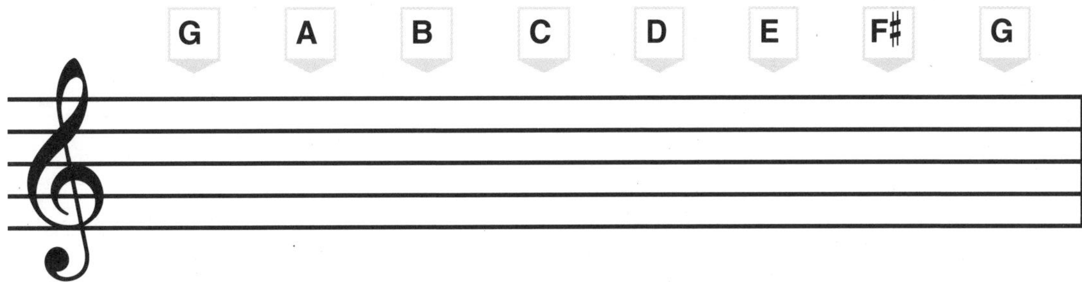

5. Write the notes of the G MAJOR SCALE in the BASS staff over the squares.
   Use WHOLE NOTES.

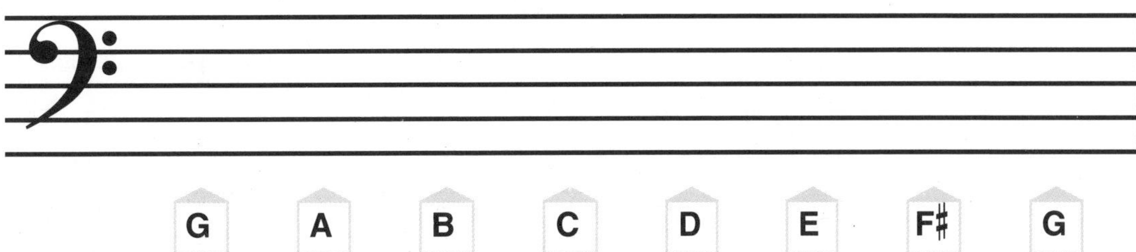

Note Review

Use with page 48.

Solve the crossword puzzle by writing the names of the notes in the squares.

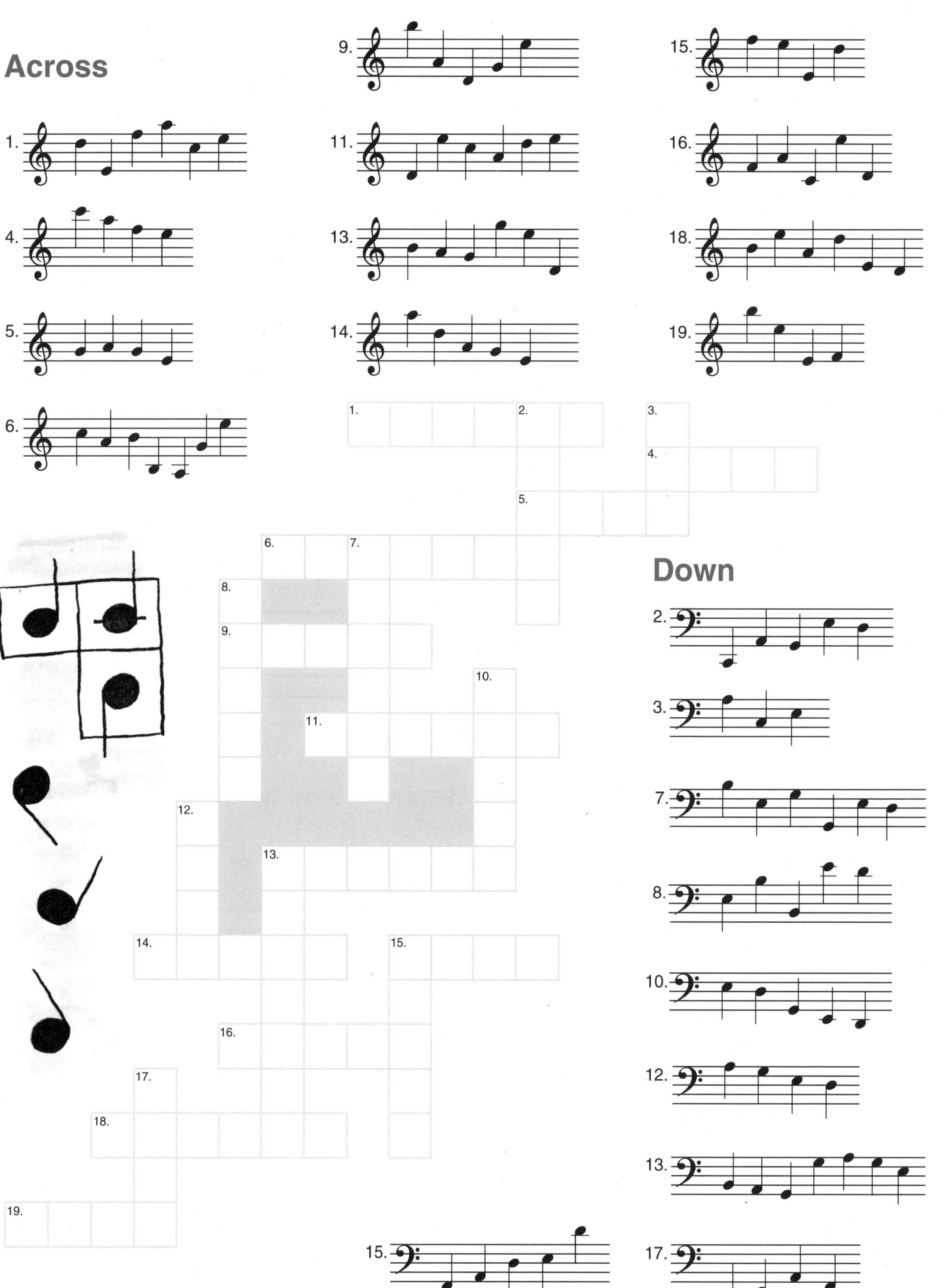

Use with page 49.

Note Review

1. Write the name of each note in the square below it—then play and say the note names.

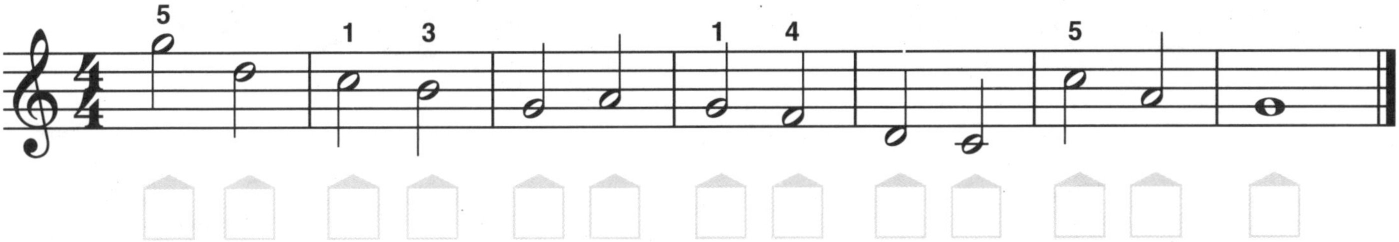

5 1 3 1 4 5

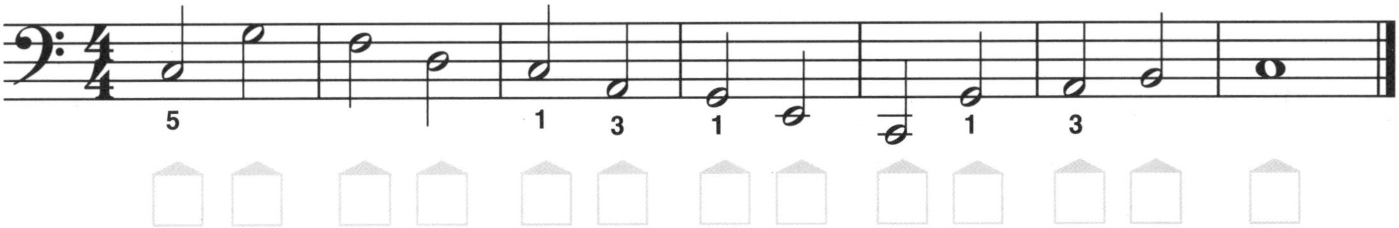

5 1 3 1 1 3

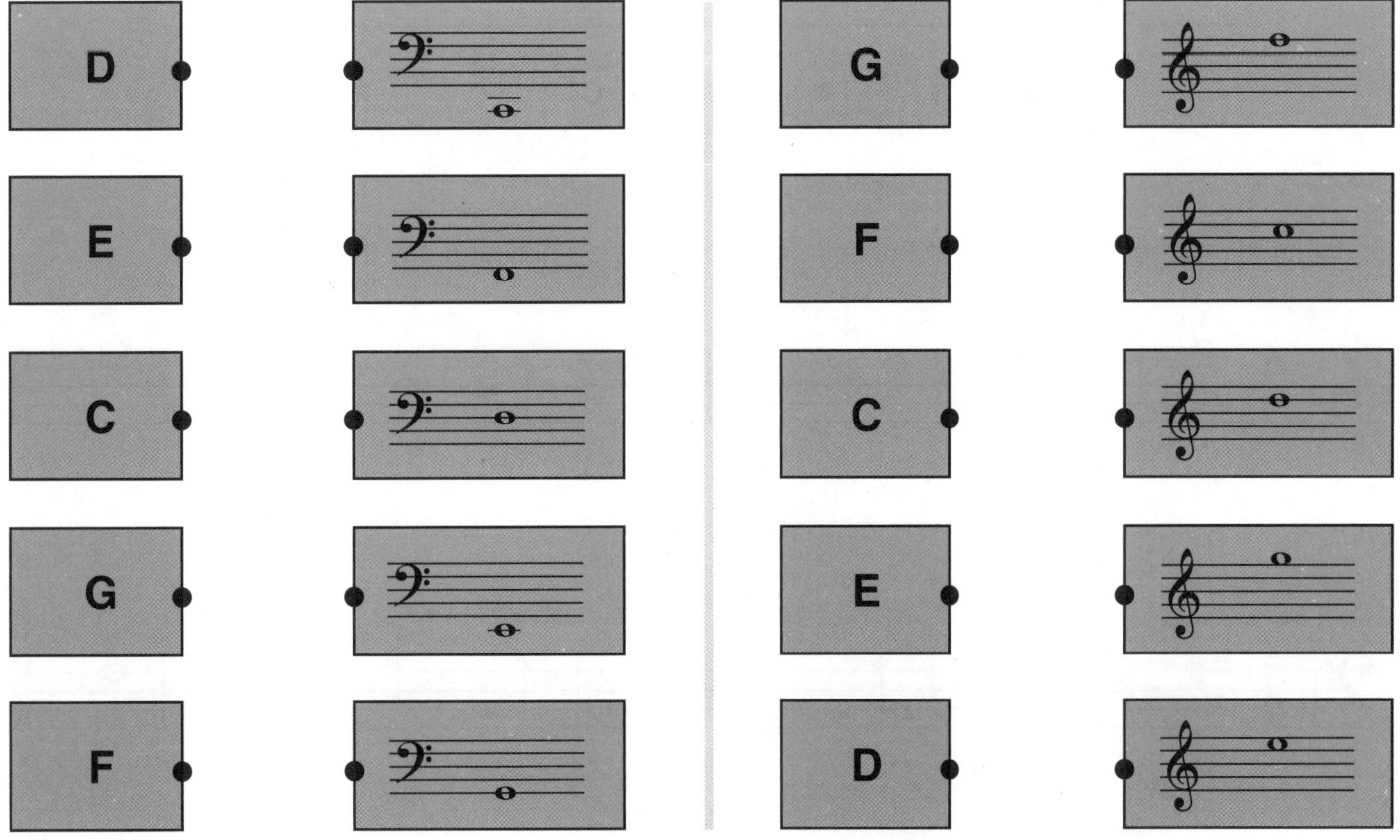

2. Draw lines connecting the dots on the matching boxes.

D

E

C

G

F

G

F

C

E

D

Use with page 50.

The F Major Scale

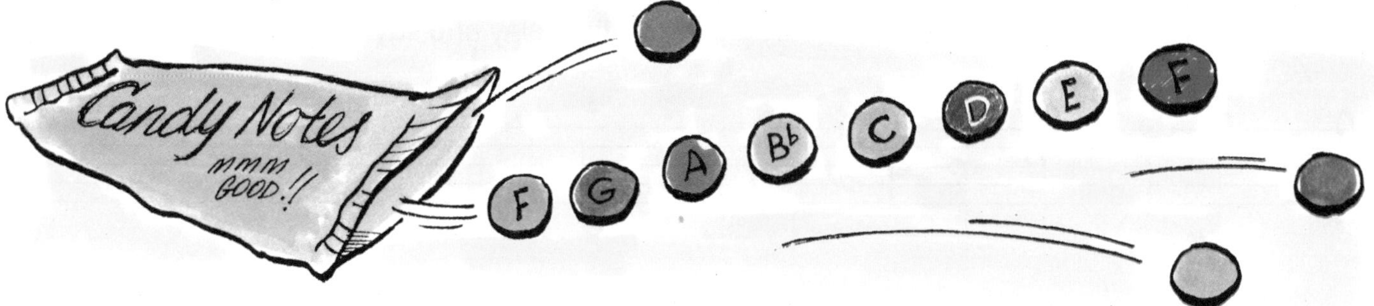

1. Write the notes of the F MAJOR SCALE in the TREBLE staff under the squares.
   Use WHOLE NOTES.

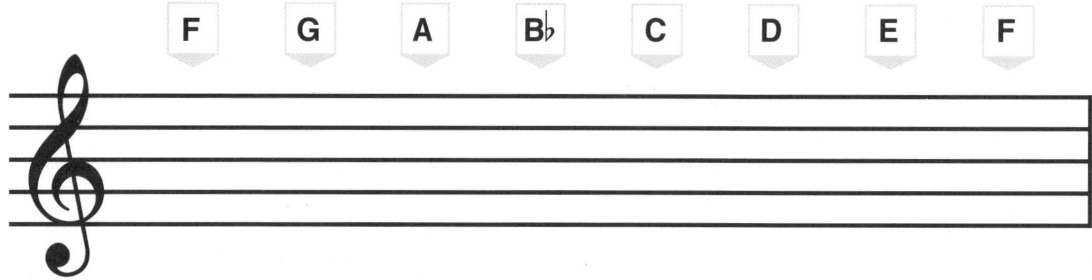

2. Write the notes of the F MAJOR SCALE in the BASS staff over the squares.
   Use WHOLE NOTES.

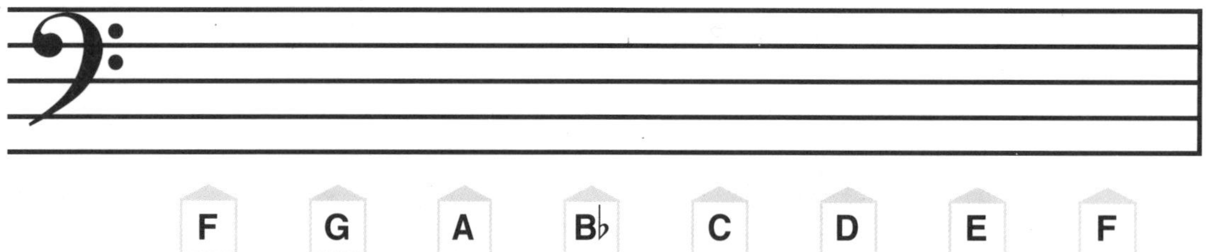

3. Write the name of each note in the square below it—then play and say the note names.

Use with page 51.

Interval Review

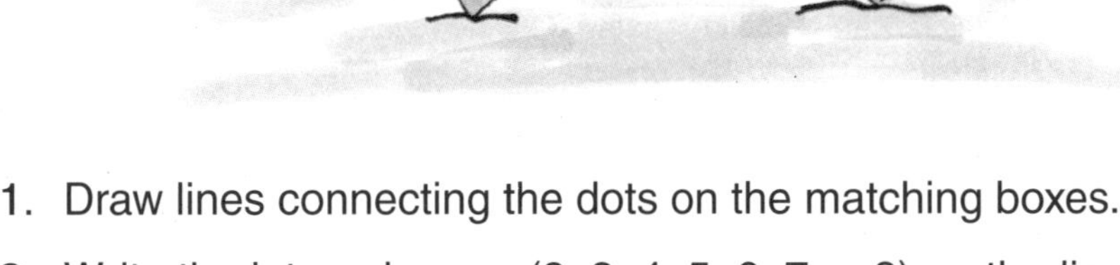

1. Draw lines connecting the dots on the matching boxes.
2. Write the interval name (2, 3, 4, 5, 6, 7 or 8) on the line.

Name	Staff	Interval
F–D		____
G–F		____
F–E		____
C–F		____
D–F		____
C–C		____
A–E		____
C–D		____

Name	Staff	Interval
C–G		____
F–F		____
A–F		____
E–B		____
C–E		____
E–F		____
F–A		____
G–A		____

Use with pages 52–53.

The Primary Chords in F Major

1. Write the names of the notes in each chord in the squares above the staff.
2. Circle the root of each chord on the staff.
3. Write the name of the chord (**I**, **IV** or **V**7) on the line below the staff.

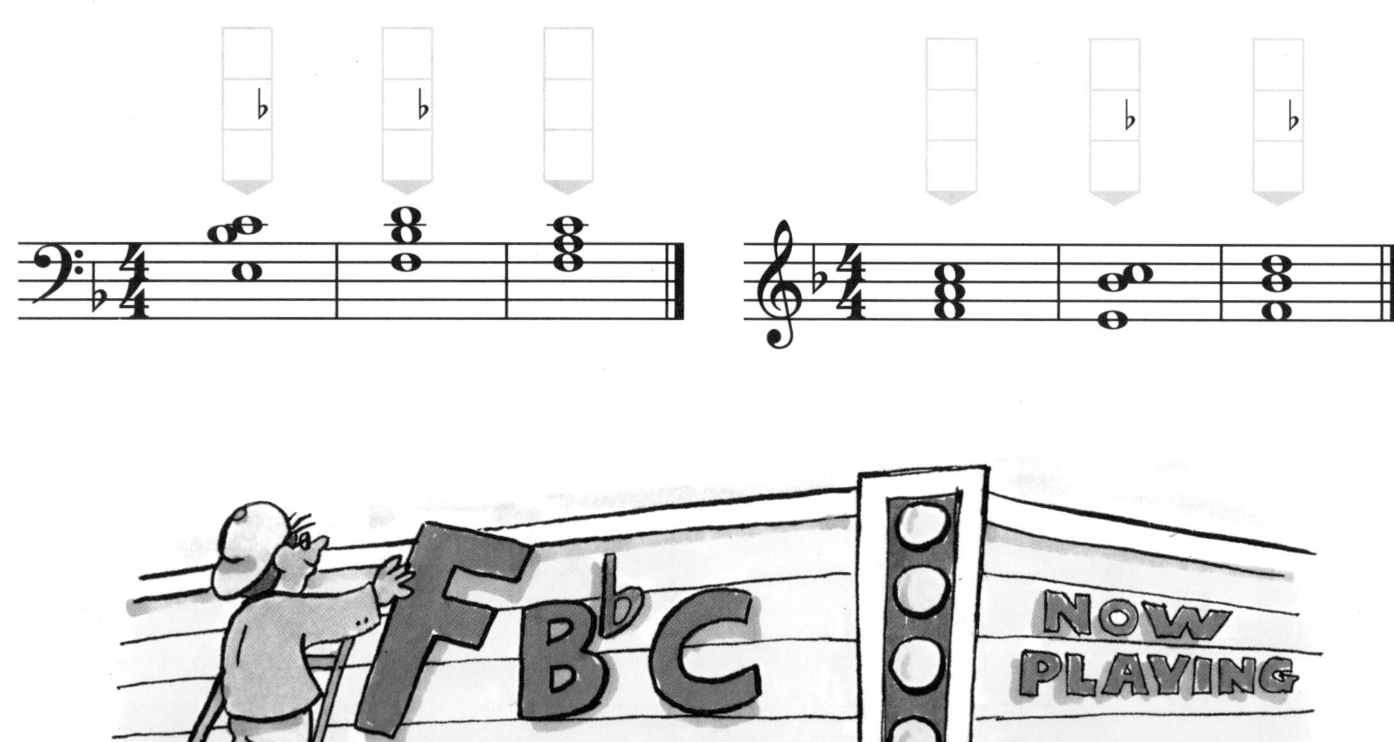

4. Draw a line from the dot on the right of each box to the dot on the left of the matching box in the next column.

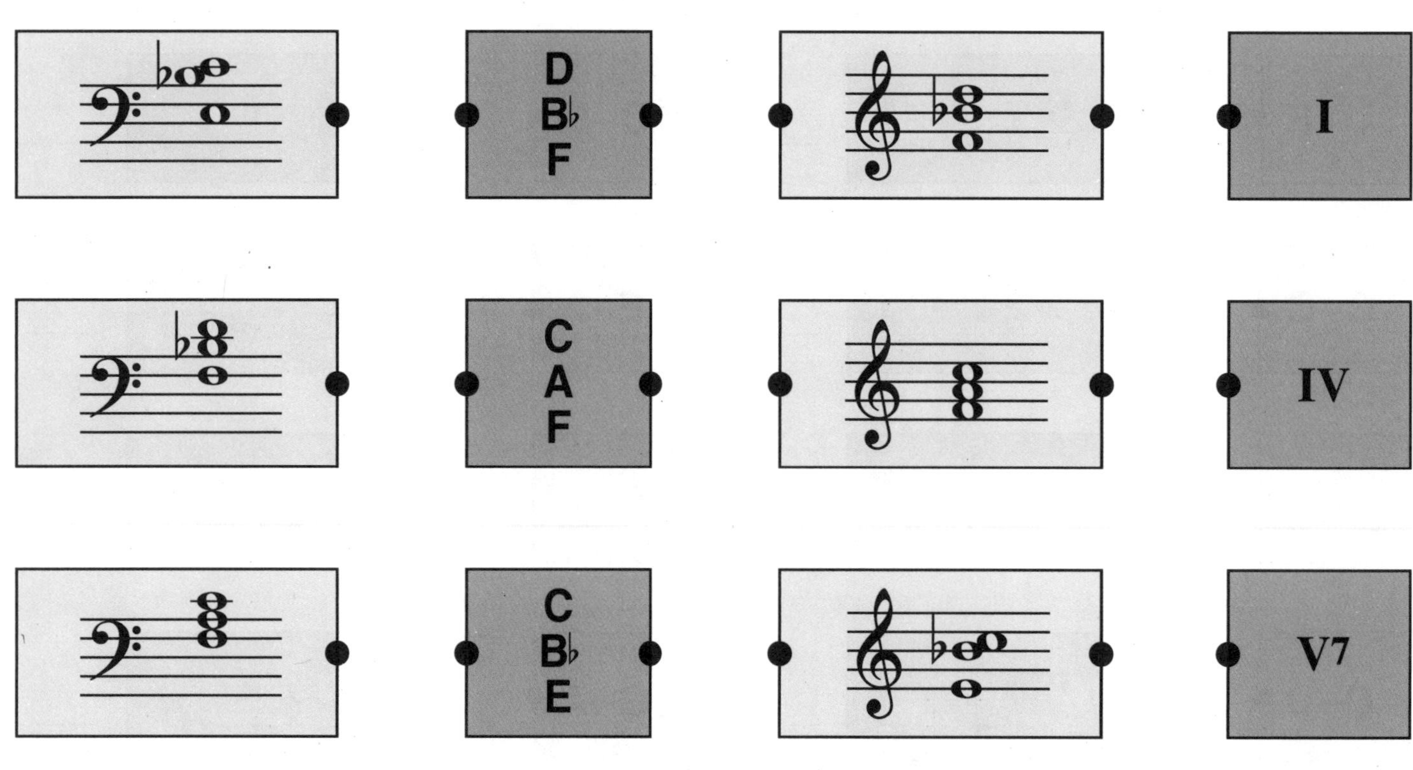

Use with page 54.

Intervals in A Minor

Circle the interval on the staff that matches the letter names.

1. **A–A**

2. **A–D**

3. **A–F**

4. **A–G♯**

5. **A–G**

6. **A–C**

7. **A–F♯**

8. **A–E**

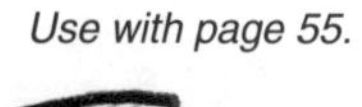

The A Harmonic Minor Scale

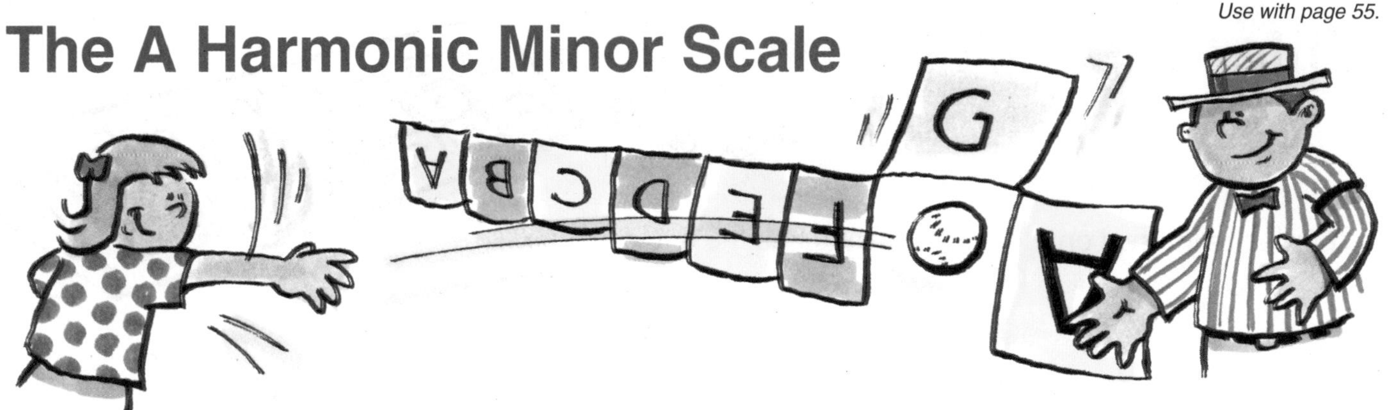

1. Write the notes of the A HARMONIC MINOR SCALE in the TREBLE staff under the squares. Use WHOLE NOTES.

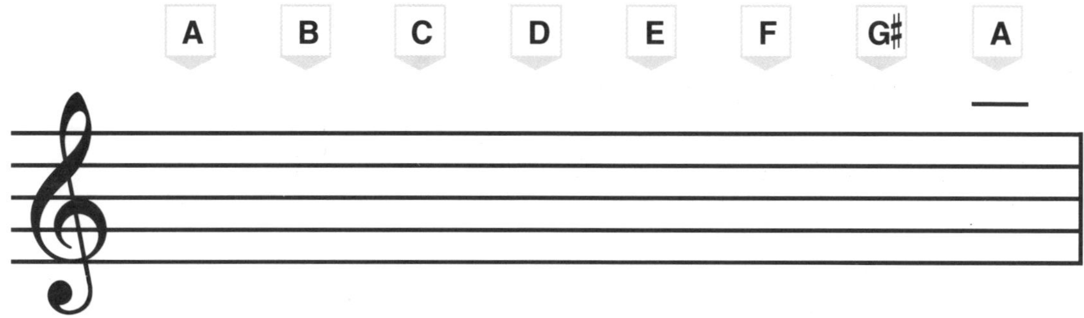

2. Write the notes of the A HARMONIC MINOR SCALE in the BASS staff over the squares. Use WHOLE NOTES.

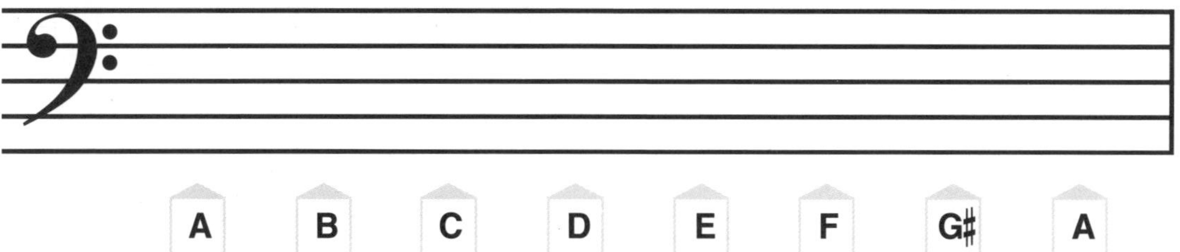

3. Write the name of each note in the square below it—then play and say the note names.

Use with page 56.

3rds and 5ths

1. Draw lines connecting the dots on the matching boxes.
2. Write the interval name on the line (M3 for major 3rd, m3 for minor 3rd, P5 for perfect 5th).

F♯ D	____	A D	____
G C	____	E♭ C	____
G E	____	E A	____
D G	____	G♯ E	____
A F	____	B G	____
B E	____	C F	____
F♯ B	____	D♯ B	____
C A	____	A♭ F	____

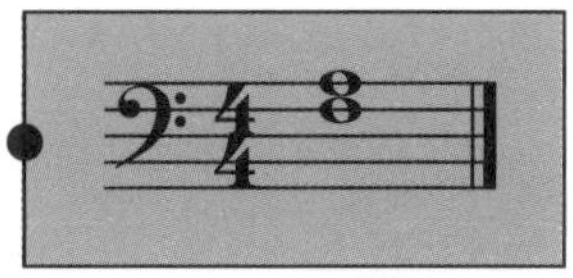

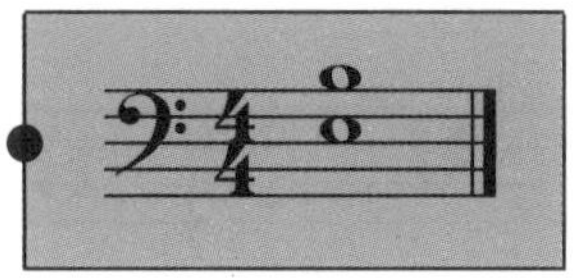

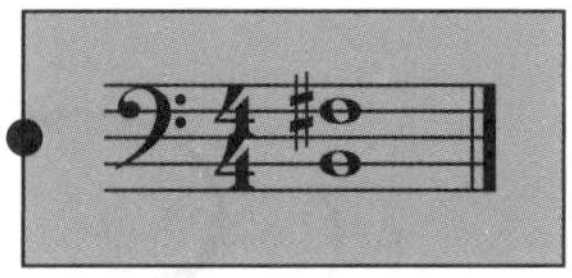

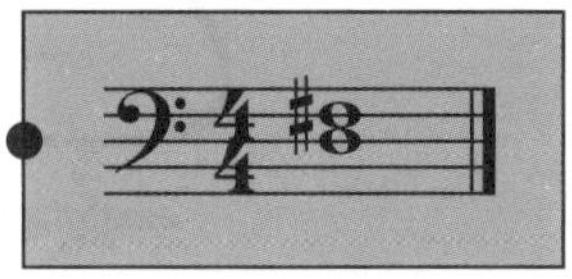

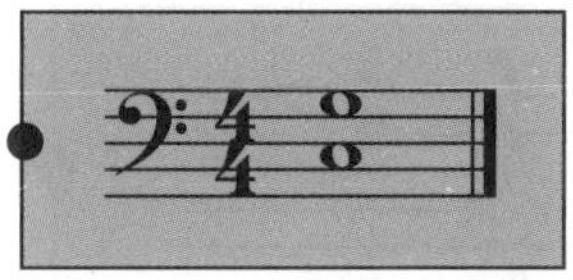

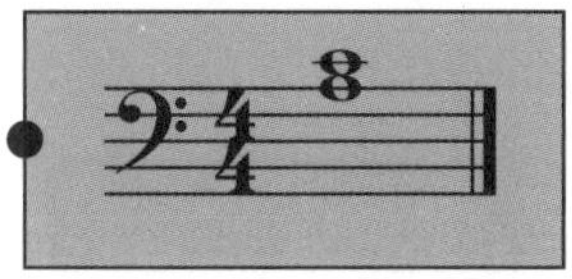

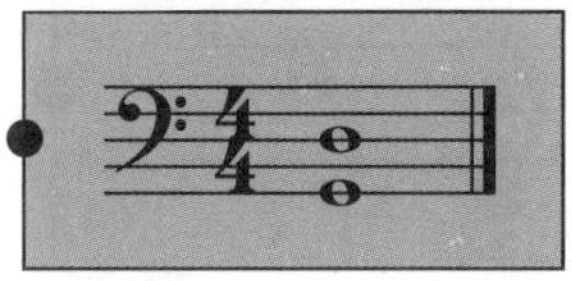

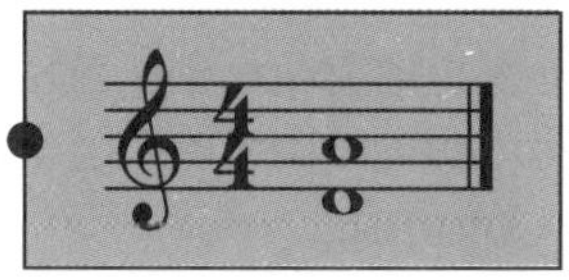

Use with page 57.

More about 3rds and 5ths

1. Write the names of the notes in the squares above the staff.
2. Write the interval name (M3 for major 3rd, m3 for minor third, P5 for perfect 5th) on the line below the staff.

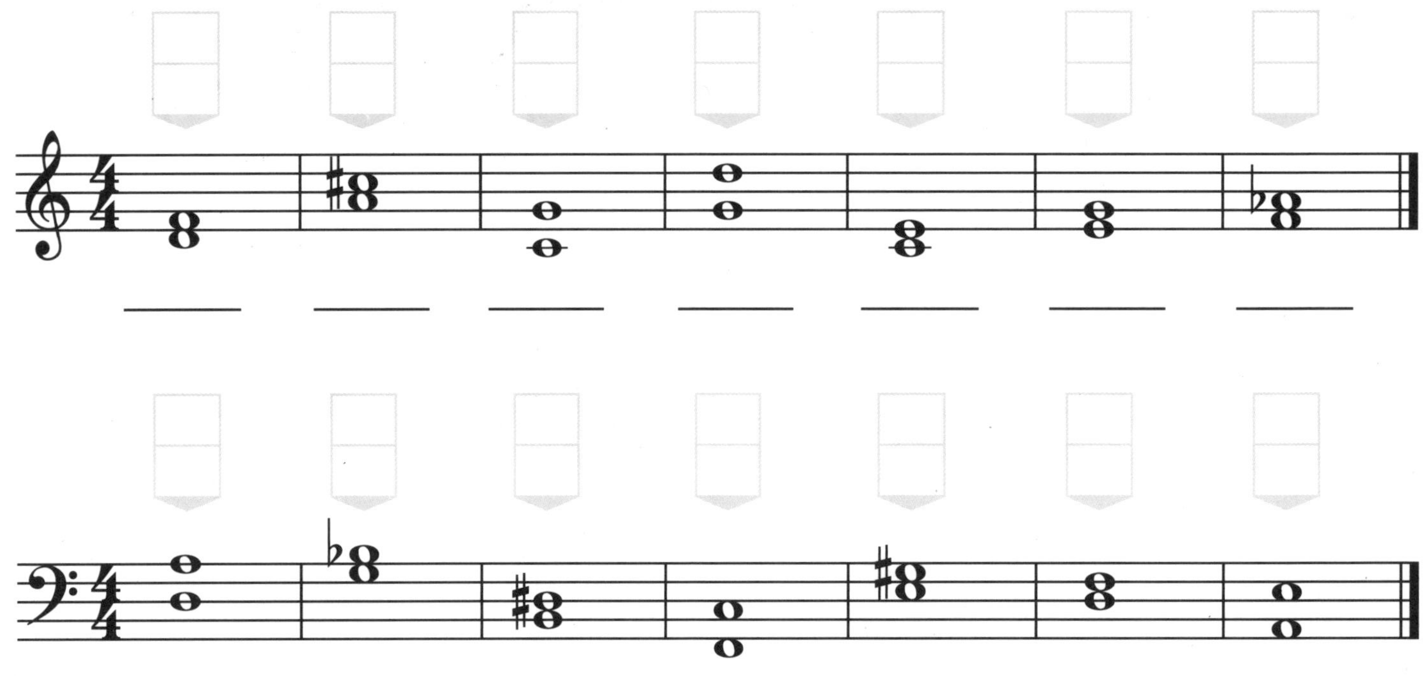

3. Draw a line from the dot on the right of each box to the dot on the left of the matching box in the next column.

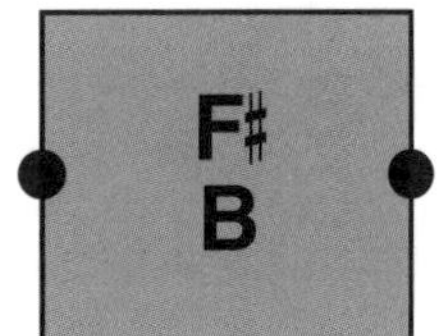

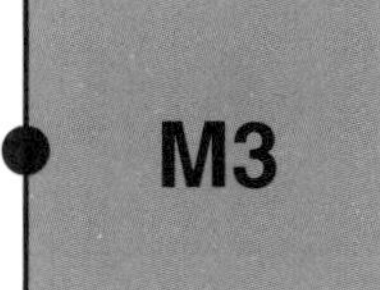

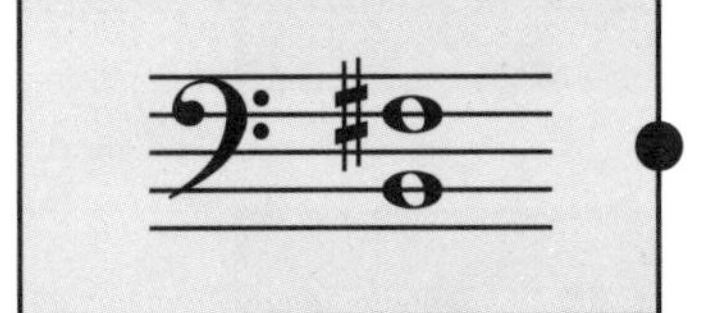

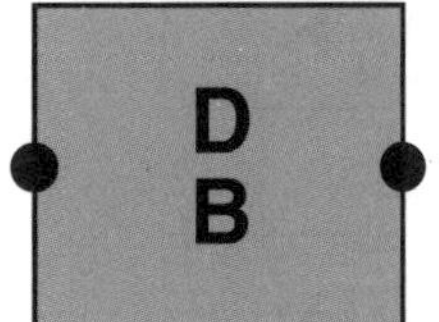

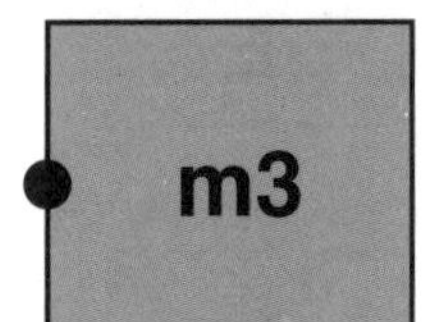

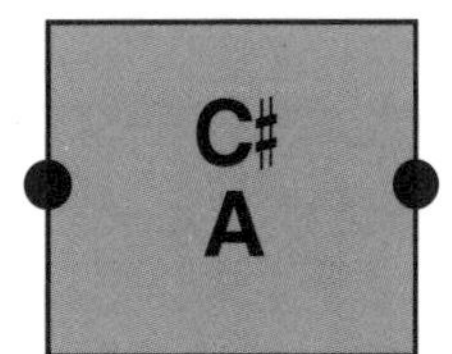

Use with pages 58–59.

Major and Minor Triads

1. Circle the triad on the bass staff that matches its name in the middle column.
2. Circle the triad on the treble staff that matches its name in the middle column.

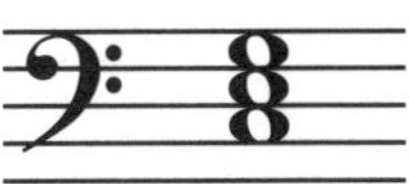 

C Major

D Minor

E Major

F Major

 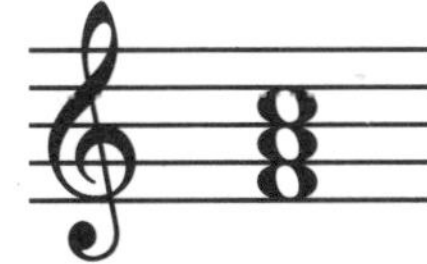

G Minor

A Minor

B Major

Use with pages 60–61.

Block Chords

Circle the block chord on the staff that matches the letter names.

1. A F♯ D

2. E C A

3. C A♭ F

4. B G♯ E

5. E C A

6. D B G

7. C A F

8. B G♯ E

Use with page 62.

The Primary Triads in Minor Keys

Remember: The three most important triads in any key are those built on the 1st, 4th & 5th notes of the scale. These are called the PRIMARY TRIADS of the key.

To find the primary triads in a MINOR KEY, the HARMONIC MINOR SCALE is used.
In the A HARMONIC MINOR SCALE, the 7th note (G) is made SHARP, as an ACCIDENTAL.

1. Circle the 1st, 4th and 5th notes of each of the scales below.
   These notes are the roots of the primary triads.

Lower case Roman numerals are used for minor triads (**i** and **iv**).
Upper case Roman numerals are used for major triads (**V**).

To make the chord progressions easier to play and sound better, the **iv** and **V** chords may be played in other positions by moving one or more of the higher chord tones down an octave.

The **i** chord is played in ROOT POSITION: | The top note of the **iv** chord is moved down an octave: | The 2 top notes of the **V** chord are moved down an octave:

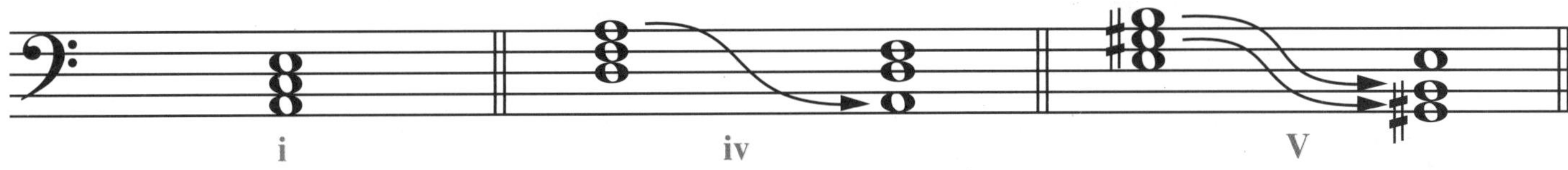

When a triad is not in root position, the ROOT is ALWAYS the *upper note* of the interval of a 4th!

2. Write the names of the notes in each chord in the squares above the staff.
3. Circle the root of each chord on the staff.
4. Write the name of the chord (**i**, **iv** or **V**) on the line below the staff.

i iv V

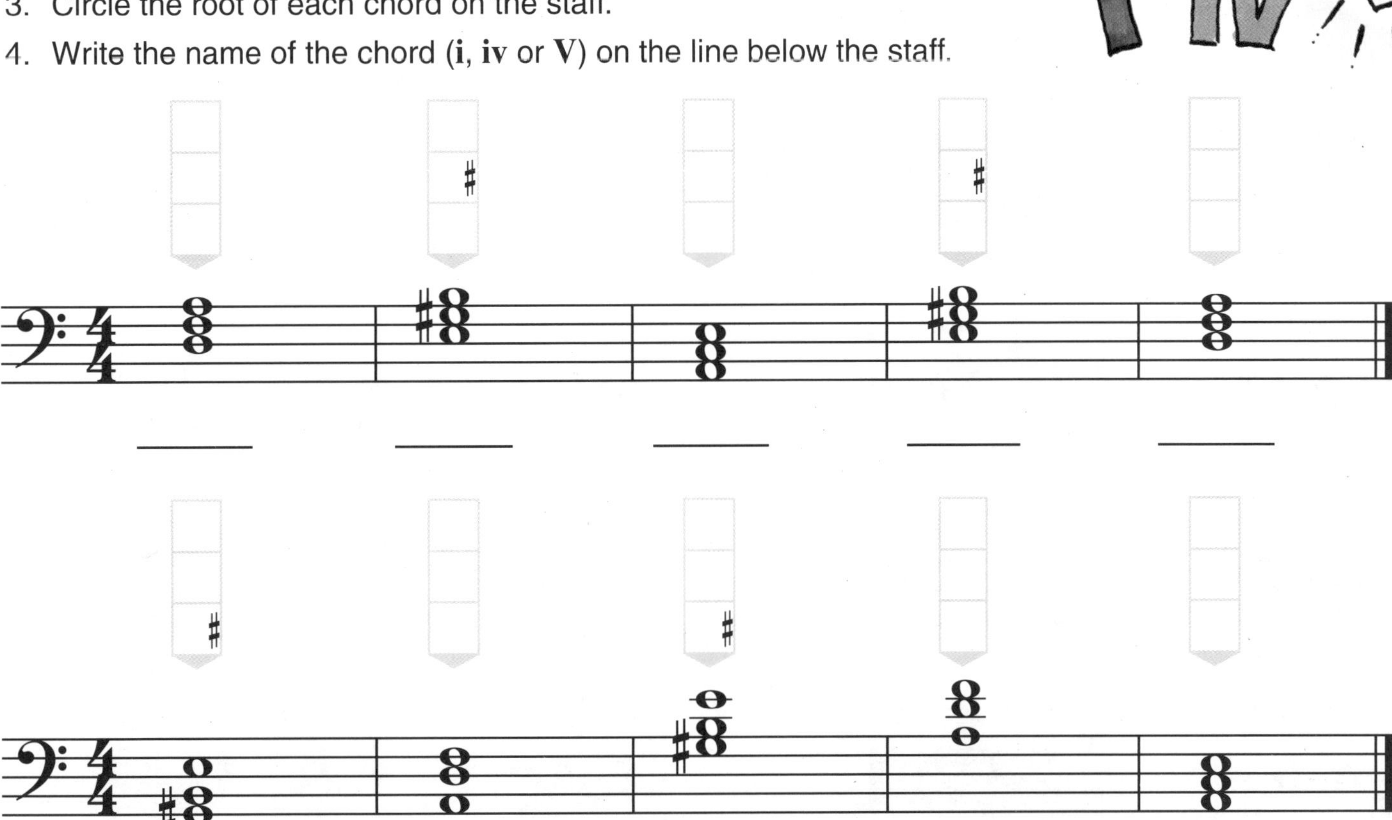

Use with page 63.

Interval Review

1. Draw lines connecting the dots on the matching boxes.
2. Write the interval name (3, 4, 5, 6, 7 or 8) on the line.

Interval	Answer
A–A	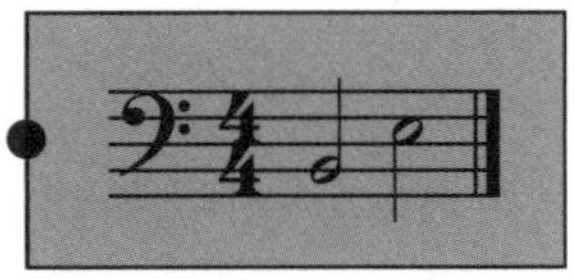 ____
F–A	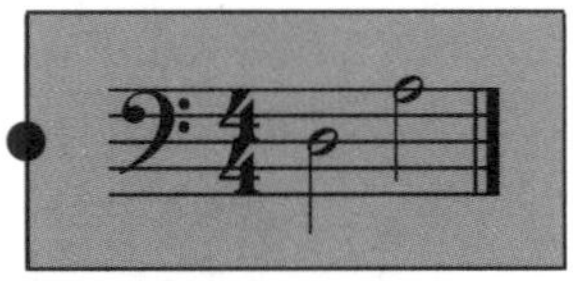 ____
B–E	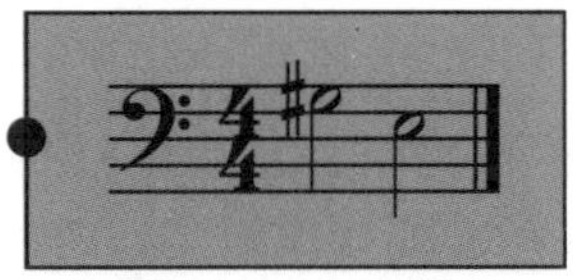 ____
A–E	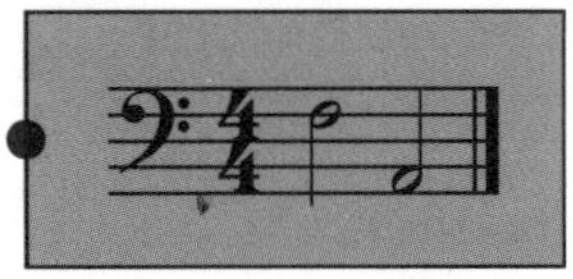 ____
D–A	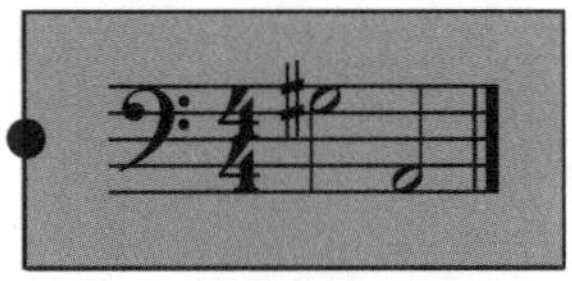 ____
G♯–A	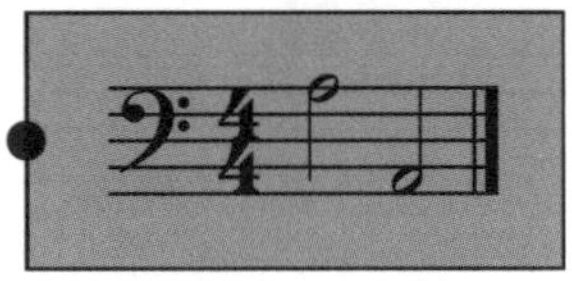 ____
G♯–E	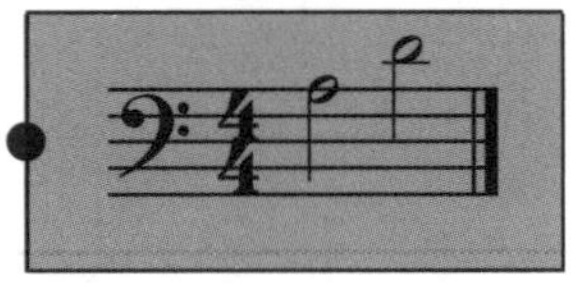 ____
A–D	 ____

Interval	Answer
C–E	 ____
C–A	 ____
E–G♯	 ____
C–A	 ____
D–G♯	 ____
A–G♯	 ____
A–A	 ____
E–A	 ____

Use with pages 64–65.

The Primary Chords in A Minor

1. Write the names of the notes in each chord in the squares above the staff.
2. Circle the root of each chord on the staff.
3. Write the name of the chord (**i**, **iv** or $\mathbf{V^7}$) on the line below the staff.

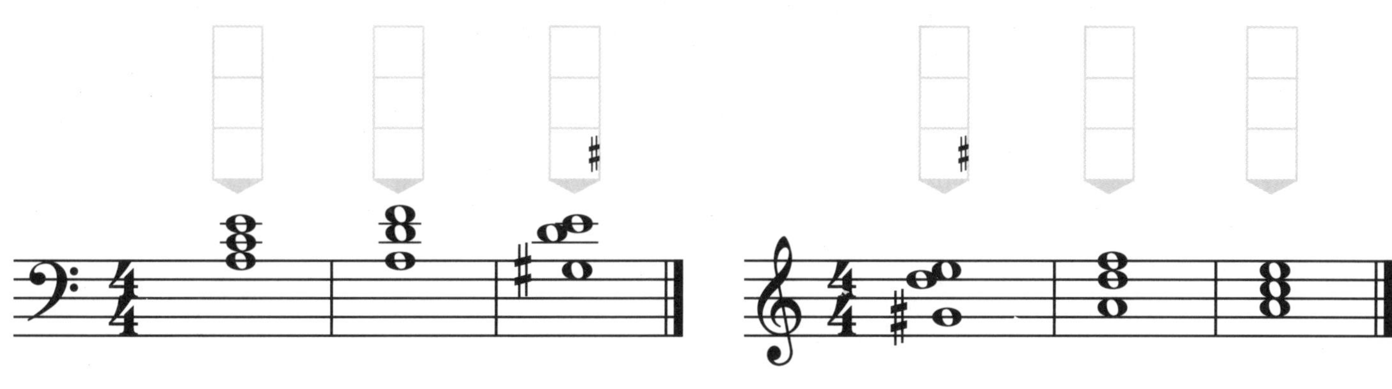

4. Draw a line from the dot on the right of each box to the dot on the left of the matching box in the next column.

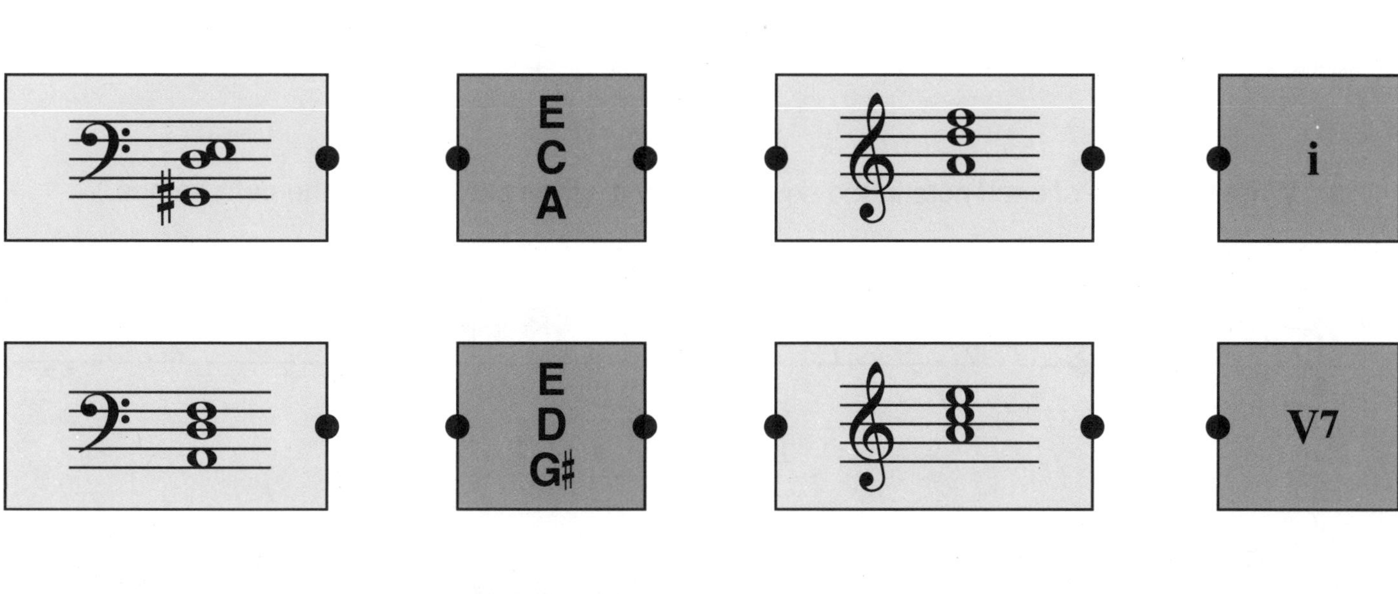

Use with page 66.

The D Harmonic Minor Scale

1. Write the notes of the D HARMONIC MINOR SCALE in the TREBLE staff under the squares. Use WHOLE NOTES.

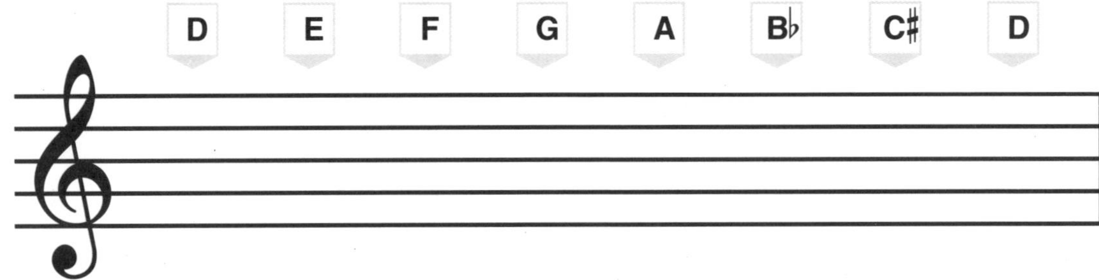

2. Write the notes of the D HARMONIC MINOR SCALE in the BASS staff over the squares. Use WHOLE NOTES.

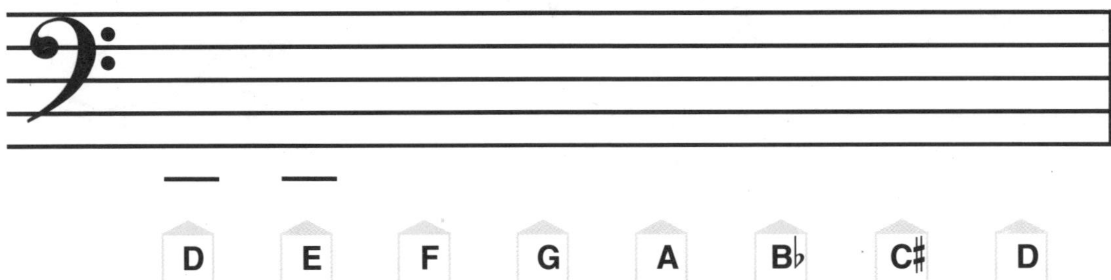

3. Write the name of each note in the square below it—then play and say the note names.

Use with page 67.

Interval Review

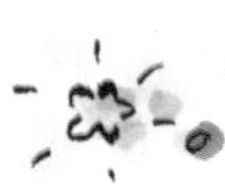

1. Write a half note DOWN from the given note in each measure to make the indicated melodic interval.
2. Write the name of each note in the square below it.

3. Write a whole note BELOW the given note to make the indicated harmonic interval.
4. Write the names of the notes in the squares below the staff. Write the name of the lower note in the lower square; the name of the higher note in the higher square.

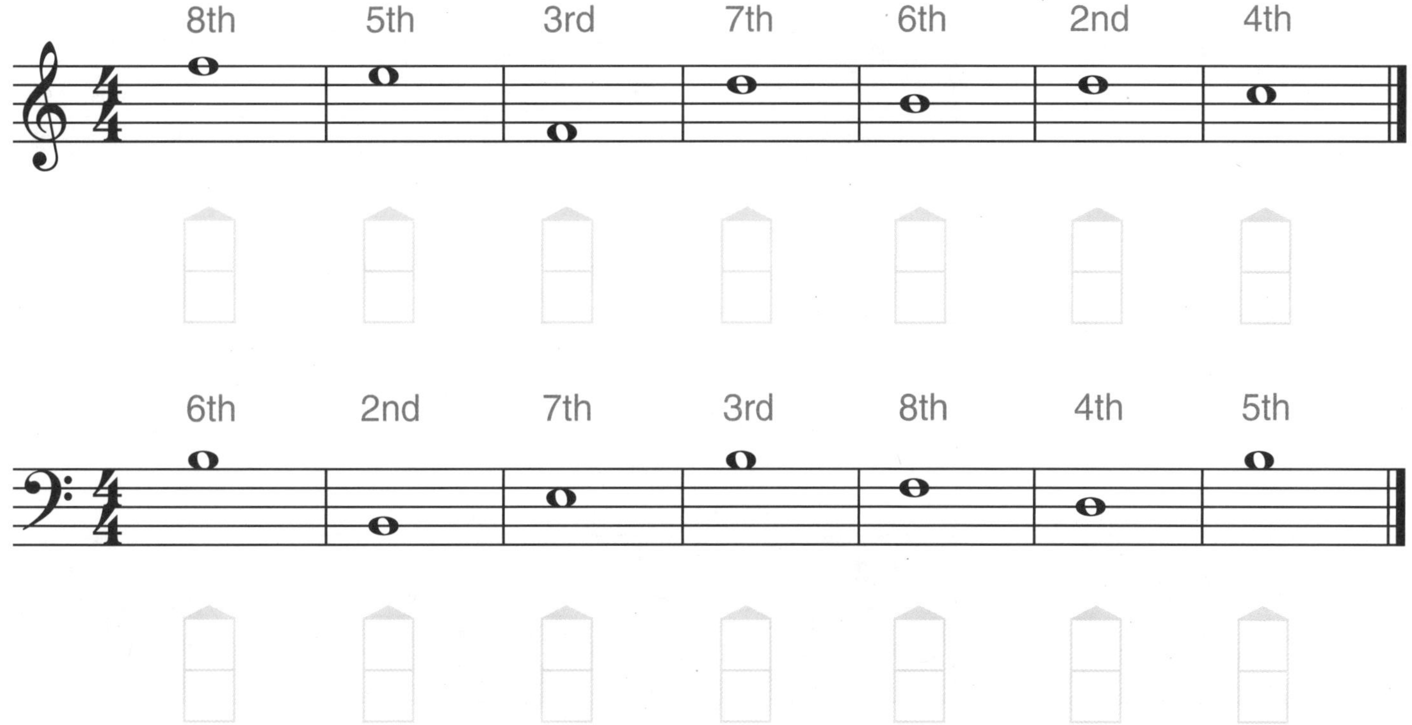

Use with pages 68–69.

The Primary Chords in D Minor

1. Write the names of the notes in each chord in the squares above the staff.
2. Circle the root of each chord on the staff.
3. Write the name of the chord (**i**, **iv** or **V**^{7}) on the line below the staff.

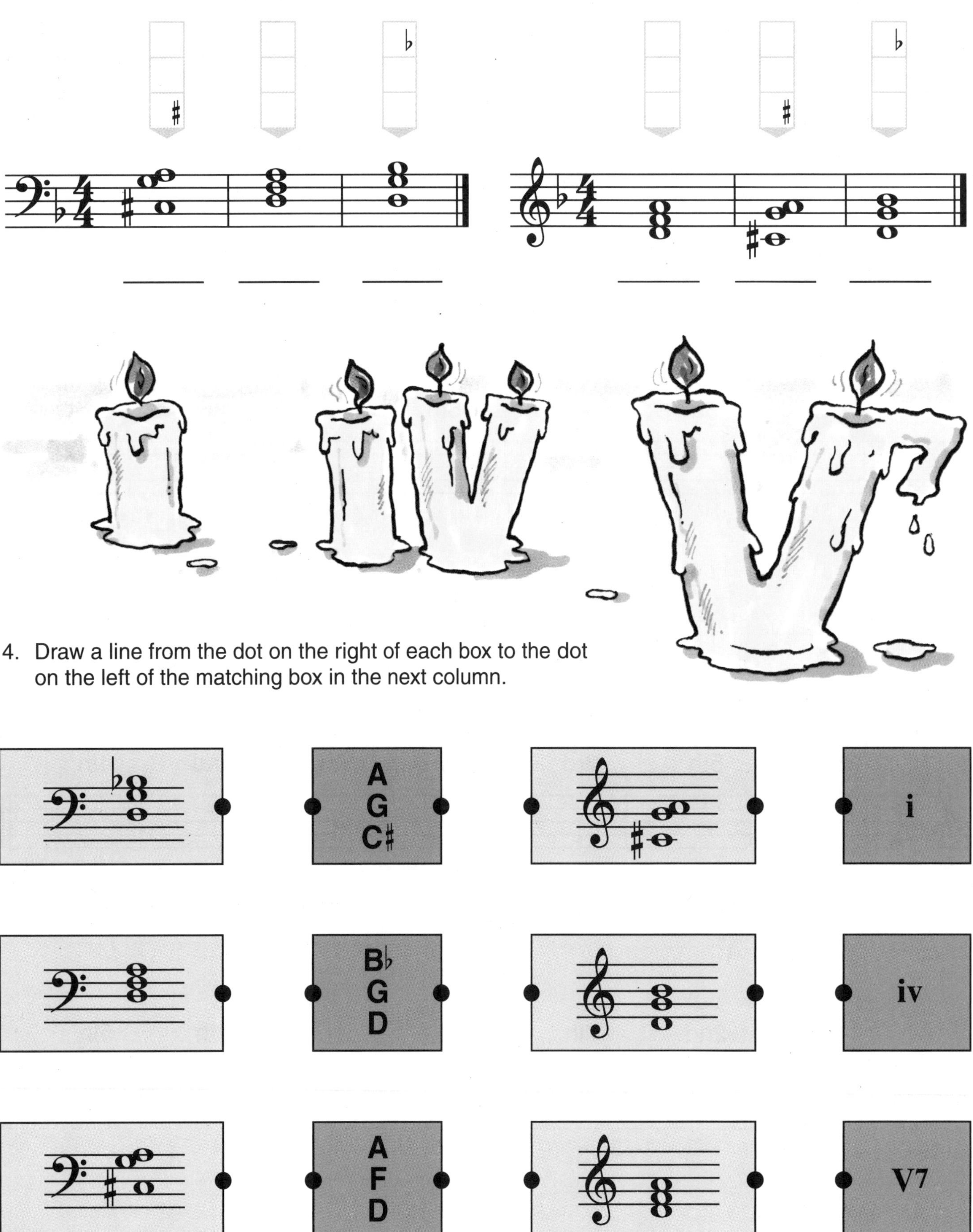

4. Draw a line from the dot on the right of each box to the dot on the left of the matching box in the next column.

Use with pages 70-71.

Melodic Patterns

Circle the melodic pattern on the staff that matches the letter names.

1. **C-D-C-B-C**   

2. **D-C-D-F**   

3. **B-C-B-A-B**   

4. **C-G-E-G**   

5. **C-E-G-E**   

6. **B-F-G-C**   

7. **C-E-G-C**   

8. **B-F-G-F**   

Use with page 72.

Chord Review

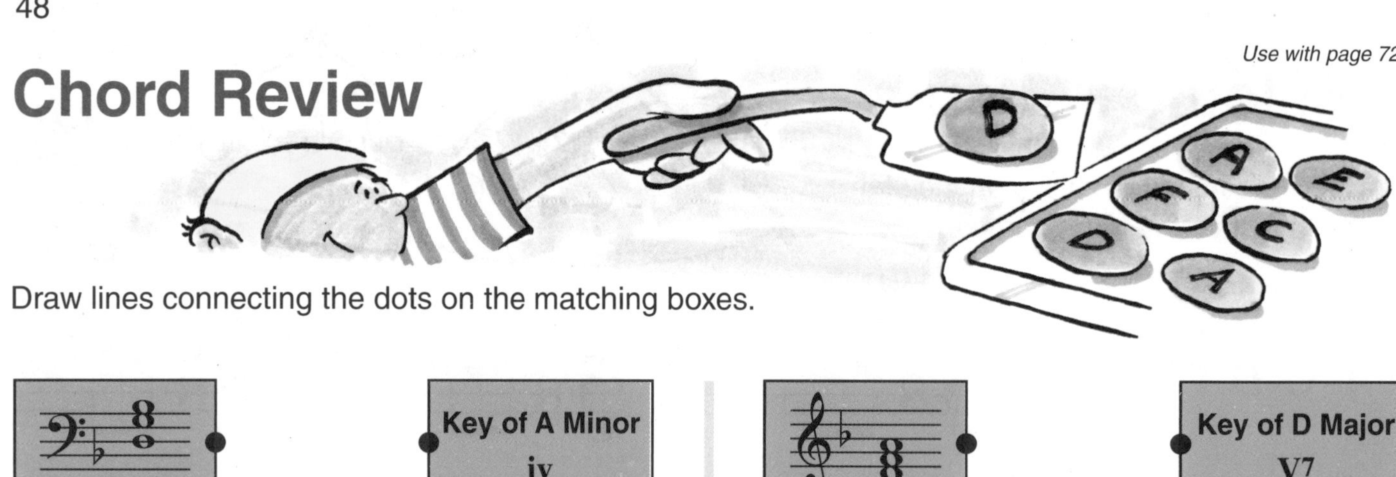

Draw lines connecting the dots on the matching boxes.

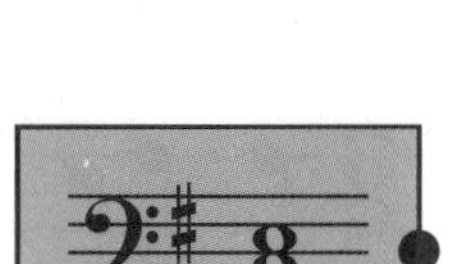	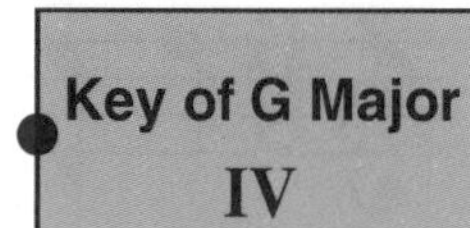 Key of A Minor iv		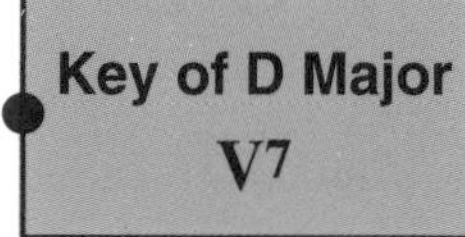 Key of D Major V7
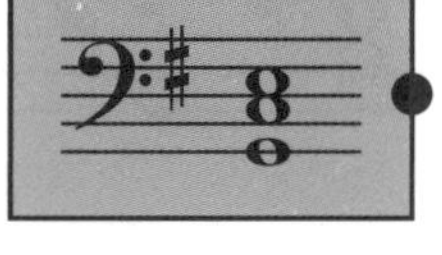	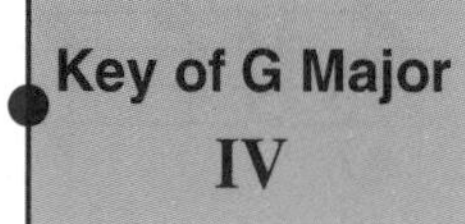 Key of G Major IV		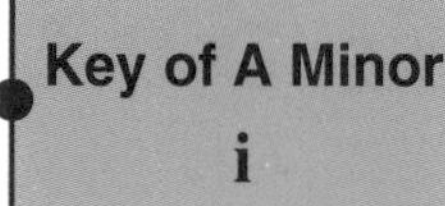 Key of A Minor i
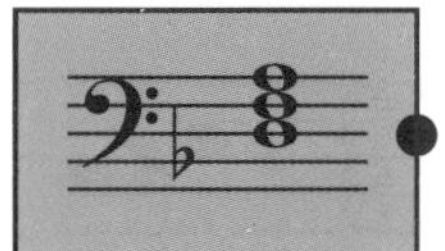	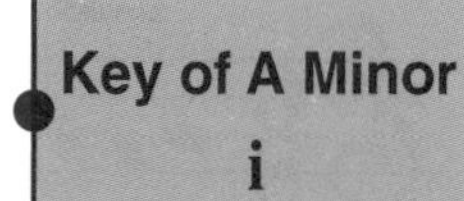 Key of A Minor i		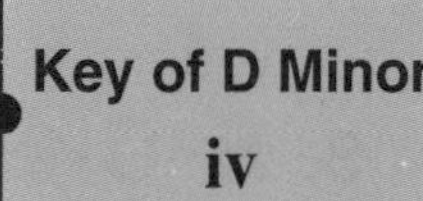 Key of D Minor iv
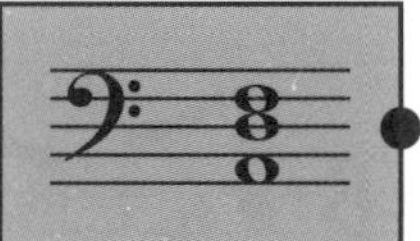	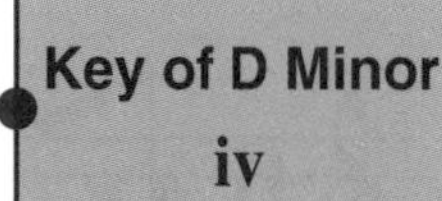 Key of D Minor iv		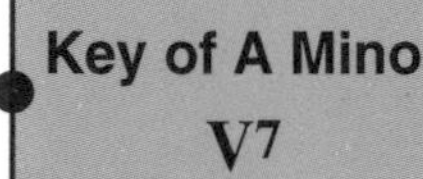 Key of A Minor V7
	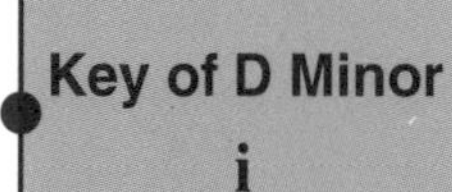 Key of D Minor i		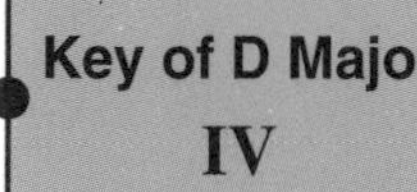 Key of D Major IV
	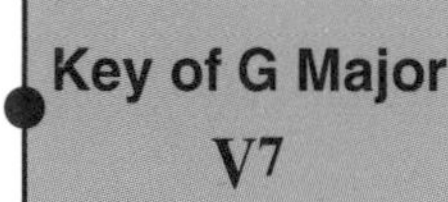 Key of G Major V7		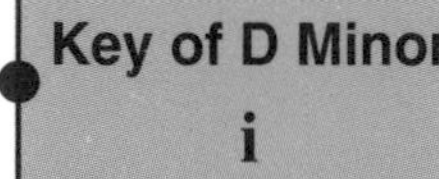 Key of D Minor i
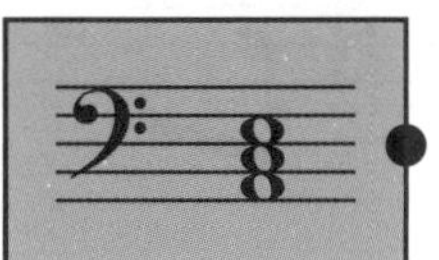	Key of A Minor V7		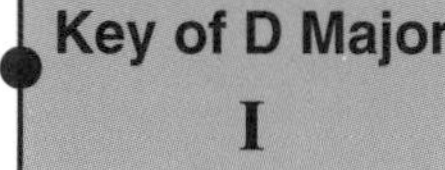 Key of D Major I
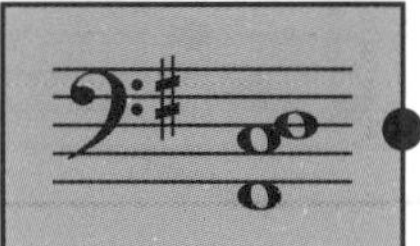	Key of D Minor V7		Key of A Minor iv
	Key of G Major I		Key of D Minor V7